Teaching Thinking Skills Across the Middle Years

A Practical Approach for Children Aged 9–14

Edited by

Belle Wallace and Richard Bentley

David Fulton Publishers

London

in association with

The National Association for Able Children in Education

David Fulton Publishers Ltd
Ormond House, 26–27 Boswell Street, London WC1N 3JZ

www.fultonpublishers.co.uk

First published in Great Britain by David Fulton Publishers 2002

Note: The right of Belle Wallace and Richard Bentley to be identified as the editors of this work has been asserted by them in accordance with the Copyright, Designs and Patents Act 1988.

Copyright © David Fulton Publishers 2002

British Library Cataloguing in Publication Data
A catalogue record for this book is available from the British Library

ISBN 1-85346-767-7

Designed and typeset by Kate Williams, Abergavenny.
Printed in Great Britain by Bell and Bain Ltd, Glasgow.

Contents

Notes on Contributors

Belle Wallace has worked with very able children for 25 years, first in an advisory capacity to Essex schools; then as a researcher and developer of a problem-solving and thinking-skills base for curriculum development. She maintains that the performance levels of all learners can be raised when they are systematically taught a range of thinking skills, and she has developed curricula internationally for disadvantaged learners. Since its inception in 1982, she has been editor of the journal *Gifted Education International*. She has published widely, served on the Executive Board of the World Council for Gifted and Talented Children, and is currently President of the National Association of Teachers for Able Children in Education (NACE), UK. Her particular interest is in working with teachers to develop their expertise in the teaching of problem-solving and thinking skills through the curriculum.

Richard Bentley was, until recently, Principal County Inspector (Curriculum and Development) with Worcestershire local education authority (LEA). Prior to this he was head teacher of a middle school. Richard's 12 years in the LEA inspectorate included middle years and middle school roles. He coordinated the LEA's support for schools in their work with more able and gifted pupils and, for several years, coordinated curricular support for pupils with special educational needs, including special schools. Richard was involved in the development of LEA initiatives in problem-solving and thinking, and this was the focus of his PhD. He has contributed to a number of publications and conferences, and is currently supporting a range of research projects in the areas of gender, high ability, thinking skills, and transition and transfer.

Elizabeth Johnstone is Teacher Adviser for Curriculum and Assessment with Worcestershire LEA. She also coordinates the LEA's support for schools in meeting the needs of their more able, gifted and talented pupils. Elizabeth is an experienced in-service education and training (INSET) provider and contributor to higher education institution (HEI) courses. She has published in the field of assessment and is experienced in writing training materials. Prior to her current post, Elizabeth taught in both primary and middle schools where she held senior management positions before organising LEA support for pupils with special educational needs.

Nigel Kent is Inspector for Curriculum (11–19) with Worcestershire LEA. Prior to taking up his current position he was Teacher Adviser for English. He has held senior management positions in several high schools. Nigel is also an HEI tutor, has contributed to national working parties and has published in the fields of literacy, and teaching and learning.

Within the LEA, Nigel and Elizabeth work intensively with schools to support teaching and learning initiatives; they also coordinate a number of 'best practice' research projects focusing on aspects of teaching and learning.

Jeanette Brocks is Teacher Adviser for Mathematics in Worcestershire, working with teachers and children in the diverse range of schools across the county. Since the implementation of the National Numeracy Strategy and the Key Stage 3 Mathematics Strategy, she has been involved in leading training and supporting schools as a Numeracy Consultant. Jeanette has 20 years' teaching experience in the primary and middle phases, together with coordinating mathematics in a large city junior school. Throughout her career, she has been committed to promoting mathematics as a subject that is achievable, relevant, challenging and fun.

Melisa Bayliss graduated from University of Sussex in 1995. She is currently Mathematics Coordinator in a large Worcester primary school, where she led the implementation of the National Numeracy Strategy. Melisa has a special interest in making mathematics exciting and accessible to children across the whole ability range.

Sue Foster-Agg has taught across all phases in a number of schools within Birmingham and Worcestershire LEAs, often in areas of social need. At present, she is head teacher of a small primary school outside Worcester. Her interest in mathematics was inspired by involvement in the then Pilot Numeracy Project.

Steve Davies has been Worcestershire's Science Inspector for the past year. Prior to this he taught for 22 years in secondary schools in Leicester, Marlborough and finally Redditch, where he taught physics and science, and in addition was assistant head teacher. His interests while teaching were astronomy and developing holography in schools.

Rashu Rosso has been Science Coordinator at a large middle school in Bromsgrove for two years, having previously taught in another 9–13 middle school within the same LEA. The pyramid of schools in which she works has for some time used Cognitive Acceleration through Science Education (CASE) material, and it was through this involvement that her interest in thinking skills developed.

Lucy Bell-Scott has taught for three years in an expanding village school on the outskirts of Worcester. She recently successfully completed a Teacher Training Agency (TTA) Level 3 Primary Science course. As part of this work she was introduced to the TASC Wheel, and was struck by the clear links between this approach and the process skills of science.

Jane Finch has been a Teacher Adviser for Information and Communications Technology (ICT) in Worcestershire for ten years; prior to that she taught ICT, drama, English and mathematics in middle schools in the same LEA. She has always had a particular interest in the use of ICT to develop the wider curriculum. Jane has been involved in research in this area as part of her Master's degree and continues to develop this interest through small-scale LEA projects. Jane is the author of several KeyBytes and LightBytes interactive ICT courses. She is currently the ICT editor for Xcalibre, the Department for Education and Skills (DfES) database for resources for more able, gifted and talented pupils.

Acknowledgements

Belle wishes to thank Harvey B. Adams with whom she worked to research and develop a generic and sound theoretical framework for the development of problem-solving and thinking skills across the curriculum. We spent 15 years working with mainly disadvantaged learners to derive a problem-solving paradigm that really worked in practice to lift learners' levels of achievement so that they had the chance to maximise their potential and take their rightful place in the world.

Belle and Richard would especially like to thank colleagues in the Worcestershire Advice and Training Service for their support. They enabled teachers and advisers to attend INSET on 'Teaching Problem-solving and Thinking Skills through the Curriculum': through continued support and encouragement the schools were keen to participate in the development of the projects which are recorded in this book.

We also wish to thank all the teachers who have been members of the wider school groups: they have trialled ideas and supported the editors by being so willing to spend extra hours in preparation and evaluative discussion. Their commitment to the children in their care is generated from genuine concern, dedication and professionalism.

Thanks to the following schools for their cooperation:

- Abbey Park Middle School, Pershore

- Aston Fields Middle School, Bromsgrove

- Blessed Edward Oldcorne RC High School, Worcester

- Cherry Orchard Primary School, Worcester

- Hagley Middle School, Stourbridge

- Hallow CE Primary School, Worcester

- Northwick Manor Junior School, Worcester

- Whittington CE Primary School, Worcester

together with all those primary, middle and high schools that sent students to the Thinking and Problem-solving Skills Summer School, 2001.

And, finally, thanks to the young adolescents who have responded with excited willingness to try new ideas and ways of working. Their enthusiasm has been evident throughout all the projects and they have told us that 'we are on the right lines' when we give them ownership and responsibility for their learning, and teach them skills of 'learning how to learn' more efficiently.

For Teachers, Parents and Students

As teachers and parents, we all want the young adolescents in our care to leave the dependence of childhood and emerge as responsible and thinking young adults: we want them to create a decent world for themselves and their families and possibly to put right the mistakes that have been made in ours. Therefore it makes sense that we teach them the skills of efficient thinking and problem-solving, and give them ample practice in as many real-life and role-play situations as we can.

How do we do this? As parents, we need to *talk* to our children about the problems that are endemic in our society: we need to *share* our own problems because they know we have some! Family discussion is in short supply these days when many families are so very busy earning a living, and when many are fragmented. For many young adolescents, the current state of the world presents a frightening prospect and we need to give them the skills they need to face up to the challenges – both personal and social. And as parents, we *do* know that it is unreasonable to expect teachers to do all the work of nurturing the young!

Obviously, teachers play a vital role in the development of our children: often they are role models and mentors, and they have the task of inducting their pupils into new areas of knowledge and skills. Often, through their enthusiasm, they arouse a life interest, or lead youngsters towards acquiring the skills they need to open the door to a career path. Frequently, they support the emotional and social needs of the children in their care. And teachers take their task seriously and professionally!

Perhaps one of the greatest needs of young people is to feel self-confident and empowered: to have high self-esteem and the belief that personal and social goals can be set and achieved. In striving for this, the teaching of problem-solving and thinking skills constitutes a powerful range of tools for young people to develop and use as life tools.

Recent research shows that 'intelligence' in all its multiple aspects is the ability to solve problems: the engineer and technicians who design and build a bridge; the soccer player who learns and uses a set of strategies; the accountant who straightens out the books; the computer enthusiast who finds the 'bug' in the programme; the dramatist who sorts out the plot; the trade union leader who argues the case – every walk of life needs problem-solvers.

But we need to ask whether young people are being trained to tackle life and learning in a problem-solving way. The important and exciting truth is that thinking and problem-solving skills *can* be taught and all human beings *can* increase their mental power! Everyone's thinking capacities can be increased, and children get excited and stimulated when they realise that they are 'training the brain'.

All the projects described in this book *generated increased motivation to learn*. Youngsters in their reflective discussions of 'What and how have we learned?' all reported that they felt they had acquired key skills and wanted to go on using those skills in their learning. The projects included youngsters across the full range of abilities. Using a problem-solving and thinking skills framework provides the slower learners with the structure they need to scaffold their learning until they can be independent, while allowing the faster learners to proceed with more independent work at an earlier stage in their development. It is easier to differentiate activities when learners are working in a problem-solving framework since the problem posed and the solution required can be presented at different levels of complexity.

Parents and teachers have joint responsibility for the nurturing of the young, but we must realise, however, that it is impossible to provide the perfect environment, and children bring their own strengths and weaknesses into the arena of growth and development. Nevertheless, as parents and teachers, we can teach them a range of skills that will give them a 'strategically good chance in life'!

Introduction

REFLECT

- How many of us can say that our parents encouraged us to say what we thought, but we had to justify our views with sound reasons?

- How many of us were excluded from adult conversations because we were told that we were too young to understand?

- How many of us have sat in the classroom with our eyes open but our minds closed?

- How many of us have forgotten the notes we spent countless hours learning for our exams?

- How many of us remember the teacher who always asked 'Well, what do you think?'

As parents and teachers we all have a mixed bag of learning experiences: some empowering and never forgotten; others disabling but also never forgotten. Consequently, as parents and teachers we try to pass on to the young those empowering experiences we remember, but we try to avoid passing on those disabling experiences.

Hence the purpose of this book is to gather together a range of ideas which constitute 'good learning experiences' for children. The projects are underpinned by sound and well-researched theory of how children best learn using a problem-solving and thinking skills approach.

Although the book is mainly for teachers working within the National Curriculum Framework, parents can use the same techniques at home to help children develop a problem-solving approach for tackling any project they undertake.

The government has been urging teachers to develop 'better standards' of achievement for all pupils, but unfortunately, this has often meant that teachers have been directed to cover more content at a faster pace. However, we would argue that better standards will be achieved *and maintained* only when teachers are encouraged to work on developing problem-solving and thinking skills across the curriculum, and this learning and teaching process needs time for practice and consolidation.

Good teachers have always been concerned that their pupils were engaged in *thinking,* hence the purpose of this book is not to suggest that good problem-solving classroom practice doesn't happen; rather the purpose is to sharpen and extend that good practice. In the light of worldwide research into how we best develop children's thinking, there is new awareness of how the brain works when it is functioning efficiently. There is also evidence that 'intelligence' is not fixed and if we teach in certain ways, learners can enhance their thinking capacities.

Selecting appropriate content as the vehicle for problem-solving and thinking is obviously very important, and linking new learning to what the learner already knows is essential. We know that we must use our knowledge if we are to retain it as active knowledge. This doesn't mean that we never rote learn or watch a demonstration, or practise a set of basic skills such as tables or spelling, but it does mean that we take every opportunity to embed all learning in relevant problems to be solved and that we systematically teach the thinking skills to do that successfully. Consequently, the intended aims of this book are to:

- provide an accessible and 'hands-on' manual of ideas for teachers and parents to use in order to develop children's thinking capacity;

- provide guidance on how to extend the current work being carried out in schools in an incremental and time-effective way, so that standards are raised across the school;

- share practical ideas that have been developed by teachers for teachers;

- show examples of children's work from a problem-solving and thinking-skills framework;

- provide a sound theoretical base for the teaching of problem-solving and thinking skills that will justify good practice; and,

- present information that is quickly absorbed through a series of mindmaps that give an overview of important points for planning and decision-making.

Don't Work Harder! Work Smarter!

BELLE WALLACE

We need *thoughtful learning*. We need schools that . . . focus not just on schooling memories but on schooling minds. . . . We need 'a literacy of thoughtfulness'. We need educational settings with 'thinking-centred' learning, where students learn by thinking through what they are learning about.

(Perkins 1992: 7)

We can think of 'smart schools' . . . as exhibiting three characteristics:

Informed. Administrators, teachers, and indeed students in the smart school know a lot about human thinking and learning and how it works best. And they know a lot about school structure and collaboration and how it works best.

Energetic. The smart school requires spirit as much as information. In the smart school, measures are taken to cultivate positive energy in the structure of the school, the style of administration, and the treatment of teachers and students.

Thoughtful. Smart schools are thoughtful places, in the double sense of caring and mindful. First of all, people are sensitive to one another's needs and treat others thoughtfully. Second, both the teaching/learning and the school decision-making processes are *thinking centered.*

(Perkins 1992: 3)

PURPOSE

More than ever before, schools are aware that they need to work 'smarter' rather than 'harder' for two fundamental, common-sense reasons. Firstly, the daily demands on teachers mean that there is very little energy left at the end of the day to work any harder! Secondly, we are well aware that dealing with current living and working conditions requires thinking skills and problem-solving abilities, so that we can become smarter at coping with the increasing complexities that bombard us.

Hence the purpose of this text is not to suggest 'yet another initiative' that we must take on board, but to engage in a reflective audit of what we already do well, and then to consider ways of extending our good practice. This book is the second in a series based on the development of thinking and problem-solving skills across the curriculum (see Wallace 2001). The generic principles of working in a thinking skills paradigm are essentially the same, hence some of the core diagrams and teaching principles are repeated in this first chapter; but the *application* of the principles will be different for each Key Stage. Each subsequent chapter will focus on topics and activities relevant to learners at the end of Key Stage 2 and the beginning of Key Stage 3. There is a special reason for this emphasis: namely, the national concern over the apparent 'dip' in pupils' achievement as they move from one Key Stage to another. Transition from one stage of schooling to the next always needs to be effected carefully and thoughtfully, but the transfer from primary to secondary school is particularly problematic with regard to continuity and avoidance of repetition.

The writers thought that in looking at middle schools we could show the transition from the more 'generalist' teaching common in the primary phase to the more 'subject specialist' approach in the early secondary phase. In addition, using examples of pupils' work we could show the level of challenge that Year 7 pupils can manage. However, this is not to ignore the difficulty that secondary schools face when beginning to work with pupils from a wide range of feeder primary schools. To ease the discontinuity between Key Stages 1 and 2, many secondary schools are developing stronger working links with the primary phase: detailed portfolios of pupils' work are being passed on to secondary phase teachers and the assessment of primary pupils' levels of achievement is comprehensive and informative, making it easier for Key Stage 3 teachers to effect a smoother transition of pupils emerging from Key Stage 2.

We would emphasise, however, that the most important factor in easing the dichotomy between Key Stage 1 and 2 lies in schools working within a thinking-skills framework. This inevitably creates greater opportunity for differentiation of lesson activities, since the thinking-skills paradigm embedded in this text essentially means that teachers and pupils work together to identify appropriate and varying starting points for groups of learners.

It is important to clarify the thinking-skills rationale that underpins the approach used throughout this text. The comments opposite and overleaf were raised by teachers during discussion on IN-SET days across the country. Reflect on this discussion and discuss any additional questions you think of with a group of colleagues.

I have always asked the pupils to think! I constantly ask questions to make sure the pupils understand.

Yes, we agree that teachers are concerned that pupils are thinking, but perhaps there is a need to examine and sharpen our classroom practice. More than ever before, the complexity of modern life demands problem-solving and thinking skills.

But only the brightest pupils will ever be able to think logically at a high level. Most pupils are lazy and don't want to think for themselves. In any case, getting them to think about behaving decently is more important these days.

Intelligence is not a fixed commodity and with appropriate teaching, all pupils can become better thinkers. Most pupils have never had the chance to work systematically on developing their capacity to think more effectively. With help, all pupils are capable of reasoned decision-making. We need to model thinking skills in the classroom and this not only supports the slower learners but also provides the faster learners with the skills they need for more independent learning.

But some children inherit the capacity to think and solve problems. It's in their genes and they thrive on the challenge!

It's quite true that we all are genetically different but a good 'thinking-skills diet' helps us to maximise our mental potential just as a good 'food diet' maximises our physical potential. It's getting the right balance between 'nature' and 'nurture' that's critical. We can actively develop pupils' minds through the right kind of teaching: teaching pupils to use a range of thinking skills and learning strategies rather than telling them what to think.

Some people recommend special lessons for the teaching of problem-solving skills – 10 minutes a day or one lesson a week.

Well, problem-solving is not an add-on to the curriculum. It should be an integral part of the curriculum. Pupils learn thinking skills when they are embedded in relevant content and when teachers deliberately 'teach for transfer'. The best way for pupils to acquire a range of skills and strategies is to first embed them in real-world scenarios with which they can identify, and then to call upon the use of these skills in other contexts.

But the National Curriculum Framework is not always relevant to pupils' lives.

No, often it isn't immediately relevant to learners' lives, but as teachers, we are good at finding ways to make things relevant – finding the key to arouse learners' interest. We need to present as much content as possible as a problem to be solved – a dilemma in history, a crisis in a novel, an environmental problem in geography, an examination of evidence in science.

Some things need to be directly taught and some skills need to be practised. It can't be all problem-solving and thinking skills.

No, it can't. The way we all learn is through a balance of direct teaching, demonstration, practice, rote-learning and problem-solving. Any kind of practice needs the learners to understand the reason for it – the end product – where it is leading. Persevering with redrafting and making a final effort is made easier if the work is to be presented to a real audience.

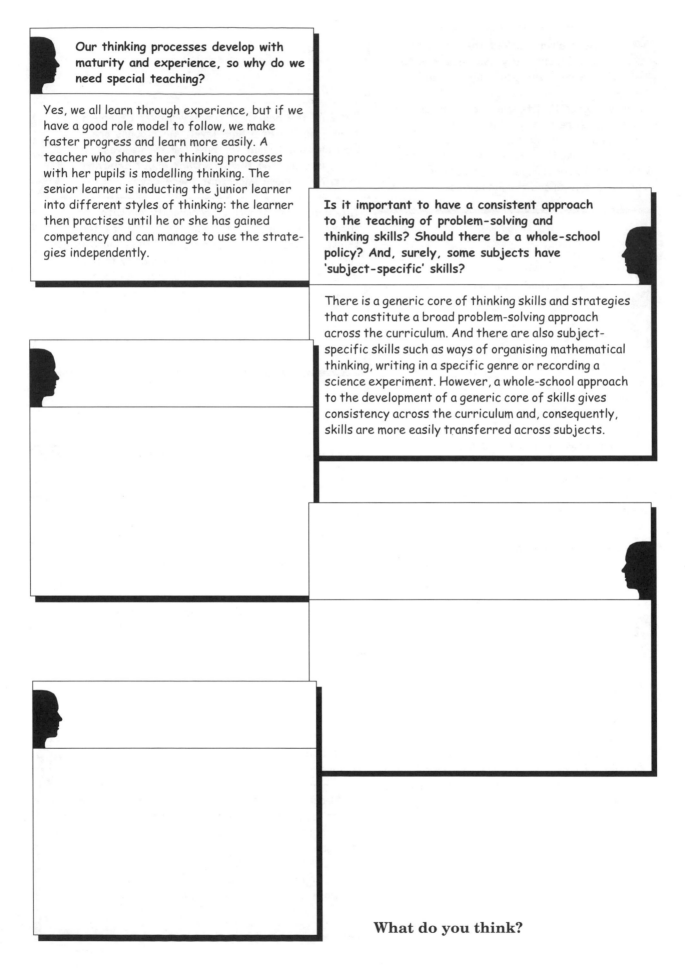

Our thinking processes develop with maturity and experience, so why do we need special teaching?

Yes, we all learn through experience, but if we have a good role model to follow, we make faster progress and learn more easily. A teacher who shares her thinking processes with her pupils is modelling thinking. The senior learner is inducting the junior learner into different styles of thinking: the learner then practises until he or she has gained competency and can manage to use the strategies independently.

Is it important to have a consistent approach to the teaching of problem-solving and thinking skills? Should there be a whole-school policy? And, surely, some subjects have 'subject-specific' skills?

There is a generic core of thinking skills and strategies that constitute a broad problem-solving approach across the curriculum. And there are also subject-specific skills such as ways of organising mathematical thinking, writing in a specific genre or recording a science experiment. However, a whole-school approach to the development of a generic core of skills gives consistency across the curriculum and, consequently, skills are more easily transferred across subjects.

What do you think?

Teachers have always been concerned that learners were 'thinking', but there are a number of perennial problems that plague us as teachers. Let's reflect on these.

> The National Curriculum Framework encompasses a massive amount of content that must be covered in a certain time.

We agree – The content in the National Curriculum Framework is extensive,

but – a great deal of it is very repetitive and many learners repeat skills and content they have already mastered. If we can reduce the amount of unnecessary repetition, then we create more time for using the content in a problem-solving way.

> There are specific subject skills and strategies that we need to teach and demonstrate and this can't always be done in a 'problem-solving' way.

We agree – Demonstration, whole-class teaching and rote-learning are important learning techniques,

but – we need to give the pupils the reasons why we use these techniques, and then embed what the learners are learning in a problem-solving exercise as often as is possible.

> I need to repeat things often because learners don't remember.

We agree – Learners do need to 'revisit' ideas as a base for further extension and they also need to practise skills in order to perfect them,

but – if we spent more time encouraging learners to reflect upon and consolidate their initial learning, then they would mentally crystallise what they had learned and would be able to recall it more easily.

> We need to repeat things because learners don't transfer knowledge and skills from one subject to another.

We agree – Transfer of knowledge and skills across subjects is a perennial problem,

but – transfer of knowledge and skills does not happen automatically. We need to consciously teach for transfer and help learners not only to see the cross-curricular links, but also the links with everyday life.

Recently, there has been the realisation in national government that the National Curriculum Framework needs to emphasise the importance of the development of problem-solving and thinking skills across the curriculum. It is apparent that many pupils are failing to reach the higher levels of achievement, especially the more able pupils who should be attaining the highest levels (Office for Standards in Education (Ofsted) 1994). Memorisation of content is not enough: the highest levels of achievement require problem-solving strategies and the thinking skills needed for dealing with higher order questions. To address this need, teachers across the country are regaining the confidence to address the *process* of the curriculum alongside the content.

However, the writers stress that 'problem-solving and thinking skills' are not just for very able pupils: 'When the fresh breeze of problem-solving and thinking skills blows, all leaves rustle.' Teaching children a range of problem-solving strategies and thinking skills enables all pupils to learn more efficiently.

Undoubtedly, good teachers have always taught with the aim of developing pupils' thinking skills, but this has often lacked coherence and consistency: and with the increase of administrative work and curriculum content, those teaching techniques that we all know are good practice have been pushed to one side. However, the climate is right for us to take stock of *how* we teach and to extend and consolidate existing good practice.

It is important to stress again that extending and consolidating a problem-solving and thinking skills approach across the curriculum provides the less able with a framework for the 'mental scaffolding' they need to develop their potential. The more able are equipped with a set of problem-solving strategies that enables them to work more independently on small-group or individual activities.

However, classroom activities that systematically develop thinking encourage and promote greater differentiation of pupil response: but when the ethos of the class is that everyone matters and can contribute to the whole, then it is acceptable to show different strengths and weaknesses.

Theoretical background to the model of problem-solving and thinking skills used throughout this text

In the mid-1980s, Belle Wallace and Harvey B. Adams surveyed the main thinking-skills packages that were already published and they visited key areas in the world where there were major thinking skills projects in operation. Then, adopting an eclectic approach that embraced the most successful elements of the range of thinking skills projects they had evaluated, they conducted an action research project with groups of disadvantaged learners and their teachers over an intensive period of ten years. Strategies and methodologies were trialled, evaluated and reflected upon by the researchers, the participating teachers, a group of educational psychologists and, importantly, the pupils. The key to the success of the action research project lay in the quality of the reflection, consequent rethinking and trialling of the thinking skills and problem-solving strategies being used. This process culminated in the publication of *TASC: Thinking Actively in a Social Context* (Wallace and Adams 1993), which sets out a generic framework for the development of a thinking and problem-solving curriculum.

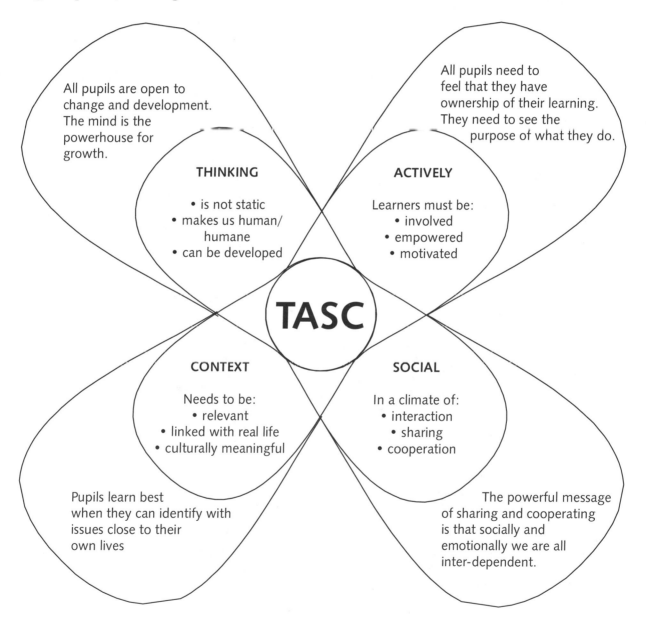

The major tenets of TASC (extended from Wallace 2000)

Would you like to add any more ideas to the basic tenets of TASC?    **REFLECT**

PURPOSE The remainder of this chapter examines the TASC framework: the theoretical base, the teaching methodology and the range of core skills and strategies that should be incorporated into any programme claiming to develop a problem-solving and thinking skills approach to the curriculum.

Understanding the theory that informs the base of TASC

COMMENT ▶ One of the most important strengths of a good teacher is a high level of emotional intelligence, which allows us to make decisions that are 'intuitive' and 'feelings based': but we need to defend those decisions with sound educational theory. Hence it is important to understand the two most important theories about how children best learn, which together form the underlying rationale from which TASC developed.

- Dig for fragments in the memory
- Recall past experiences
- Put context of learning into real-lfe issues
- Draw mindmaps to link previous learning with new learning
- Give reasons for new learning

Link all new learning with previous learning

- Fit the jigsaw pieces together
- Paint the big picture
- Show the connections
- Make it all hang together
- Make common sense of it
- Draw flow diagrams

Make concept maps or webs

How can we help children to learn?

Use extended language

- Introduce 'new' language when children understand
- Use everyday experiences to introduce technical or abstract terms
- Give lots of examples to illustrate meaning
- Build an ocean of language around an idea

Negotiate meaning

- Start from the level of children's language
- Encourage children to rephrase in their own words
- Allow time for discussion
- Let children explain to each other
- Work on communication skills

Vygotsky's 'Development of Higher Psychological Processes' (extended from Wallace 2000)

Vygotsky's 'Development of Higher Psychological Processes'

Vygotsky (1978) emphasises that pupils learn when they can recall what is already learned, and then extend their existing mental maps to accommodate new learning. The skilled teacher is adept at finding the mental 'hooks' in learners' existing learning schemes and then building from these. The new learning 'transforms' the previous knowledge, creating new networks of understanding. Vygotsky discusses the essential role of the 'senior learner' who interacts with the 'junior learner' to negotiate meaning and understanding. The senior learner provides a scaffold of support until the apprentice, junior learner demonstrates competence and independence. The major tool for interaction is language, which first needs to be grounded in the learner's informal language repertoire. This base of language then needs to be extended into the more formal and technical language needed for formal education. The teacher also needs to model styles and strategies of thinking so that the learner has a role model who both demonstrates thinking and uses thinking language. Responses, questioning techniques, attitudes, emotions and thoughts are 'caught' rather than taught, and while the home background of the learners is fundamentally influential, the ethos, atmosphere and styles of behaviour within the classroom are obviously vitally important. Most importantly, Vygotsky argues that the processes of mediation and transformation are dynamic, making the learner always open to change and growth.

Sternberg's 'Triarchic Theory of Intellectual Development'

Robert Sternberg (1985) has led the way in rethinking the whole concept of the nature of 'intelligence' and of the processes by which children are enabled to learn more effectively. He maintains that although our individual genetic inheritance varies in the range of strengths and weaknesses we possess, we can all learn to use a range of thinking skills and strategies. These make up the components of our thinking processes, which derive from a repertoire of thinking tools that enable us to use our mental capacities more efficiently. We can all learn to plan and to monitor the efficiency of our planning. We can be taught how to reflect on our thinking processes in order to improve them, and we can be assisted in the crystallisation of 'what' we know and 'how' we learn. Then using our experiences and with mediated help, we can transfer the skills and strategies we learn to new situations and contexts. These are the key processes of metacognition: reflect, consolidate and transfer. Using our thinking and problem-solving skills, we adapt to our environment; and if we are lucky enough to have the opportunity, we select the environment in which we want to function. Possibly, the highest form of human endeavour is shown when we shape the environment around us: we become the 'movers' and the 'shakers' of the world we live in.

COMPONENTIAL

Develop skills and strategies to plan, monitor, reflect and transfer

- Begin with everyday experiences
- Give skills appropriate names
- Work across the curriculum
- Give lots of practice

EXPERIENTIAL

Deal with novelty, autonomise and transfer strategies

- Deliberately 'call up' appropriate skills
- Embed skill in new situation/context
- Give relevant practice
- Discuss how else to use the skill

CONTEXTUAL

Adapt, select and shape real-world environments

- Embed skills in real-life scenarios to bring about change
- Choose relevant personal/community/school problems for learners to actively solve
- Engage learners in anticipating problems/consequences and working towards solutions

Sternberg's 'Triarchic Theory of Intellectual Development' (extended from Wallace 2000)

REFLECT

- Draw a quick mindmap of the teaching principles that characterised your own learning. Dictated notes? Rote-learning? Memorisation? Fragmentation? Teacher Talk and Test? Summary of texts?

- Now compare the teaching principles outlined in the diagrams summarising the theories of Vygotsky and Sternberg. How much of your own learning was characterised by these principles?

Considering the broad principles of the teaching methodology that underpins TASC

Outstanding teachers are 'gifted' in using their emotional intelligence: utilising both their awareness of themselves and their awareness of others to develop classroom rapport. As skilled communicators, they intuitively understand and respond effectively to the dynamics of the classroom. They are good mediators of learning, facilitators of interaction, and often they become mentors who inspire children to learn.

The purpose of this section, therefore, is not to suggest that the teaching principles of TASC are 'new' or 'revolutionary', but to invite you to reflect on, consolidate and confirm your good practice and possibly to extend your teaching strategies even further towards excellence.

PURPOSE

The spiral diagram overleaf portrays the evolutionary nature of TASC teaching principles.

- Use the spiral diagram to do a reflective audit on your own classroom practice.

- Write alongside the evolutionary stages in the spiral diagram the classroom practices you use to encourage the learners towards achieving competence in each stage of their development.

- Can you add any more ideas which in your experience lead towards successful practice?

Now compare your reflective audit with the essential teaching principles which underpin TASC (p. 13).

Reflect on the Teaching Strategies You Use in the Classroom

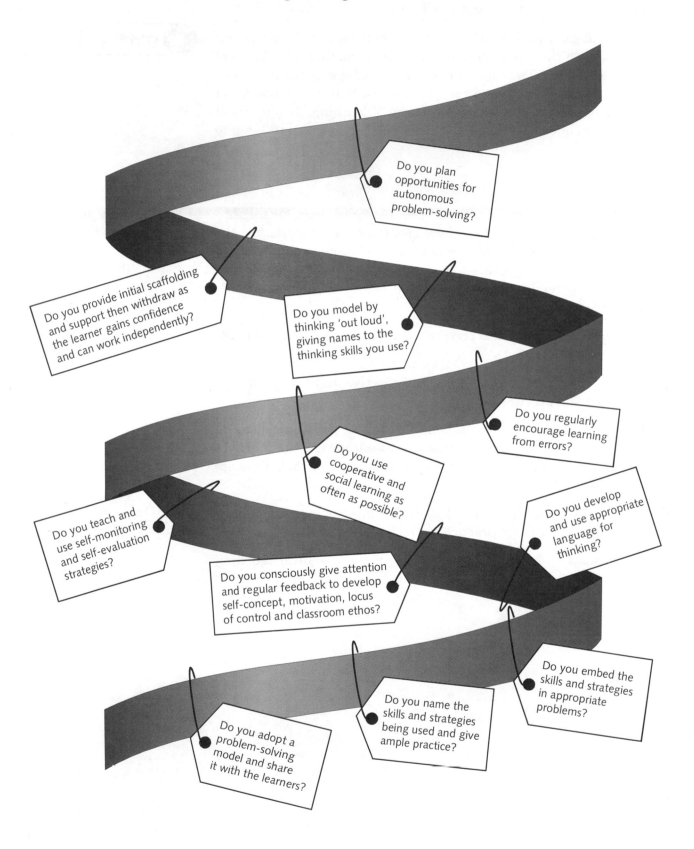

Do you plan opportunities for autonomous problem-solving?

Do you provide initial scaffolding and support then withdraw as the learner gains confidence and can work independently?

Do you model by thinking 'out loud', giving names to the thinking skills you use?

Do you regularly encourage learning from errors?

Do you use cooperative and social learning as often as possible?

Do you develop and use appropriate language for thinking?

Do you teach and use self-monitoring and self-evaluation strategies?

Do you consciously give attention and regular feedback to develop self-concept, motivation, locus of control and classroom ethos?

Do you embed the skills and strategies in appropriate problems?

Do you name the skills and strategies being used and give ample practice?

Do you adopt a problem-solving model and share it with the learners?

(Extended from Wallace 2001)

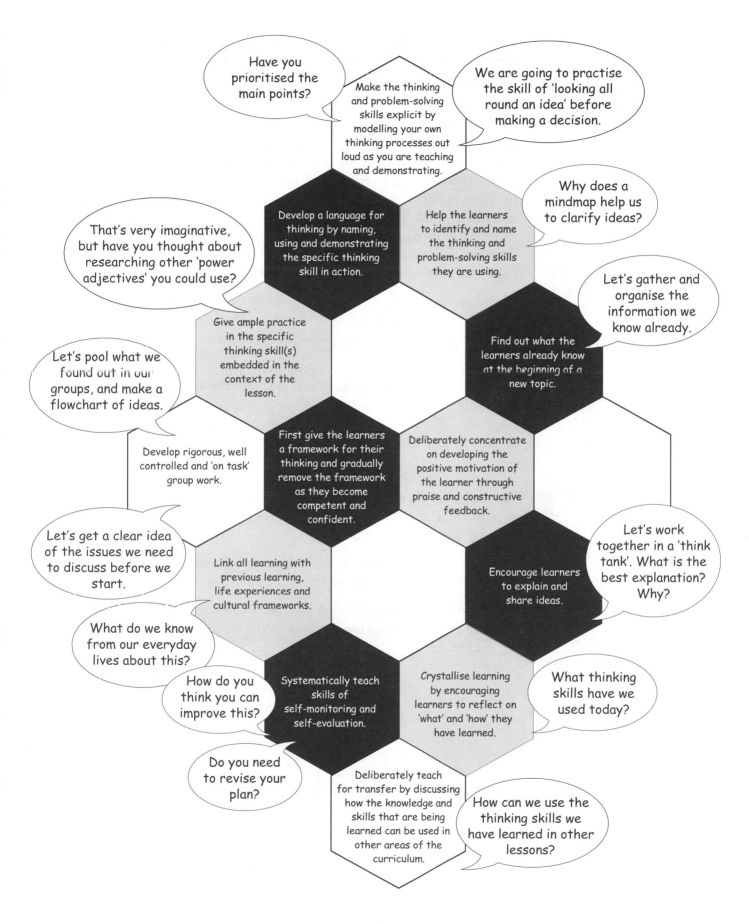

(Adapted and extended from Wallace 2001)

Putting the TASC problem-solving model and the teaching principles together in a menu of practical strategies for classroom use

Every teacher has a personal repertoire of tried and tested classroom skills and strategies that are used appropriately for differing needs and purposes. Working in a problem-solving and thinking-skills way doesn't mean that we should never teach from the front, organise purposeful learning by rote, teach specific subject skills, give opportunities for necessary practice, show by demonstration or set individual work. However, teaching problem-solving and thinking skills within subjects and across the curriculum in a planned and coherent way actively develops learners' skills of 'learning how to learn', and actively increases their mental capacities.

Always remember that any change to our usual style of teaching takes time to consolidate: but the TASC methodology is an extension of existing good practice and new strategies can be incrementally developed.

Most importantly, developing learners' problem-solving and thinking skills *initially* takes time, but once learners are familiar with the range of skills and are using them, *they learn more efficiently and we save time.*

- Refer to the extended TASC Problem-solving Wheel on pages 16–17. Use it to reflect on your repertoire of teaching skills you use regularly:

- Tick the strategies you already use and give yourself a score from 5 (use regularly) to 1 (use occasionally).

- Think about the strategies you never use and consider how you can gradually incorporate these into your repertoire of teaching skills.

Although all the stages of the TASC Problem-solving Wheel are important, there are four critical stages:

◀ COMMENT

- **Gather and organise** This stage is important because learners need to bring what they already know into their working memory ready for 'thinking, repair and extension'. This process also provides an excellent tool for assessing prior learning and enables teachers to better differentiate the learning tasks that are set. At the beginning of Key Stage 3, it is absolutely necessary to avoid the repetition of content and skills that have been learned. As well as doing this orally, learners can be given a range of key questions and tasks that reveal the level of their knowledge and understanding; but then we must be ready and willing to provide alternative learning activities for those children who demonstrate mastery.

- **Identify** Many learners get lost and lose sight of the task they are undertaking, so it is important that learners explain to each other, in their own words, the purpose of the task. It is equally important that they know and understand the criteria they will use for the evaluation of their work.

- **Evaluate** Learners need to be trained in the skill of evaluation, and they need to see examples of 'good' and 'excellent' work which clearly show evidence of the criteria they are working towards. Drafts as well as finished work need to be kept and valued as a means of showing that other pupils didn't get it right first time; also, drafts are good reminders of 'starting points' which can then be compared with 'finishing points'.

- **Learn from experience** This is a key learning point – the final reflective stage when learners crystallise and consolidate what they have learned. This is the route to the retention and transference of skills and knowledge across the curriculum. Yet it is the stage that is most commonly omitted because teachers come to the end of the lesson and the bell rings!

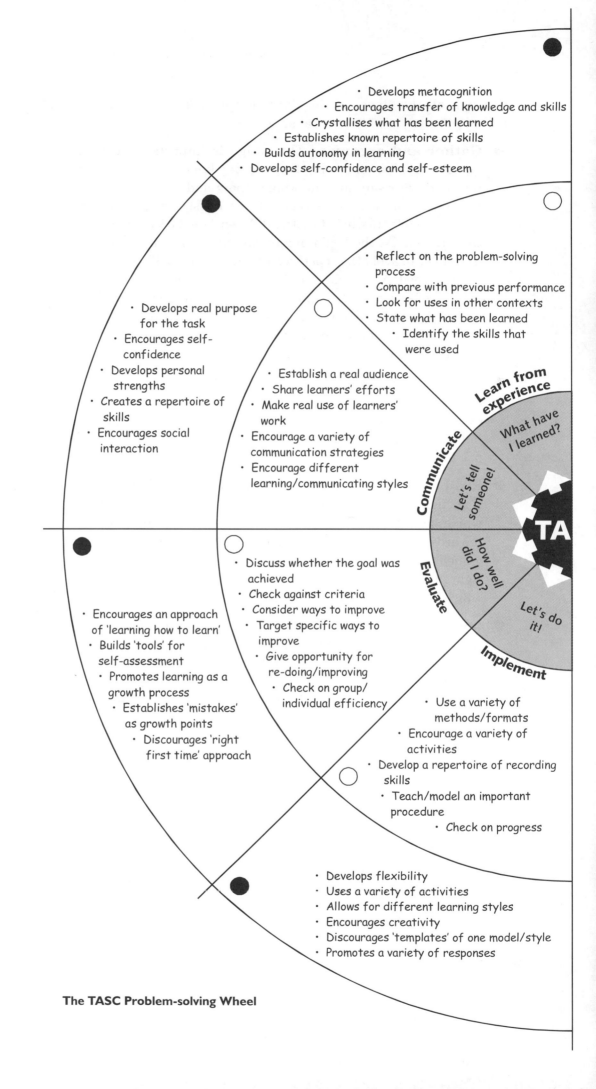

- Develops metacognition
- Encourages transfer of knowledge and skills
- Crystallises what has been learned
- Establishes known repertoire of skills
- Builds autonomy in learning
- Develops self-confidence and self-esteem

- Develops real purpose for the task
- Encourages self-confidence
- Develops personal strengths
- Creates a repertoire of skills
- Encourages social interaction

- Reflect on the problem-solving process
- Compare with previous performance
- Look for uses in other contexts
- State what has been learned
- Identify the skills that were used

- Establish a real audience
- Share learners' efforts
- Make real use of learners' work
- Encourage a variety of communication strategies
- Encourage different learning/communicating styles

Learn from experience

Communicate

What have I learned?

Let's tell someone!

Evaluate

How well did I do?

TA

Let's do it!

Implement

- Discuss whether the goal was achieved
- Check against criteria
- Consider ways to improve
- Target specific ways to improve
- Give opportunity for re-doing/improving
- Check on group/individual efficiency

- Encourages an approach of 'learning how to learn'
- Builds 'tools' for self-assessment
- Promotes learning as a growth process
- Establishes 'mistakes' as growth points
- Discourages 'right first time' approach

- Use a variety of methods/formats
- Encourage a variety of activities
- Develop a repertoire of recording skills
- Teach/model an important procedure
- Check on progress

- Develops flexibility
- Uses a variety of activities
- Allows for different learning styles
- Encourages creativity
- Discourages 'templates' of one model/style
- Promotes a variety of responses

The TASC Problem-solving Wheel

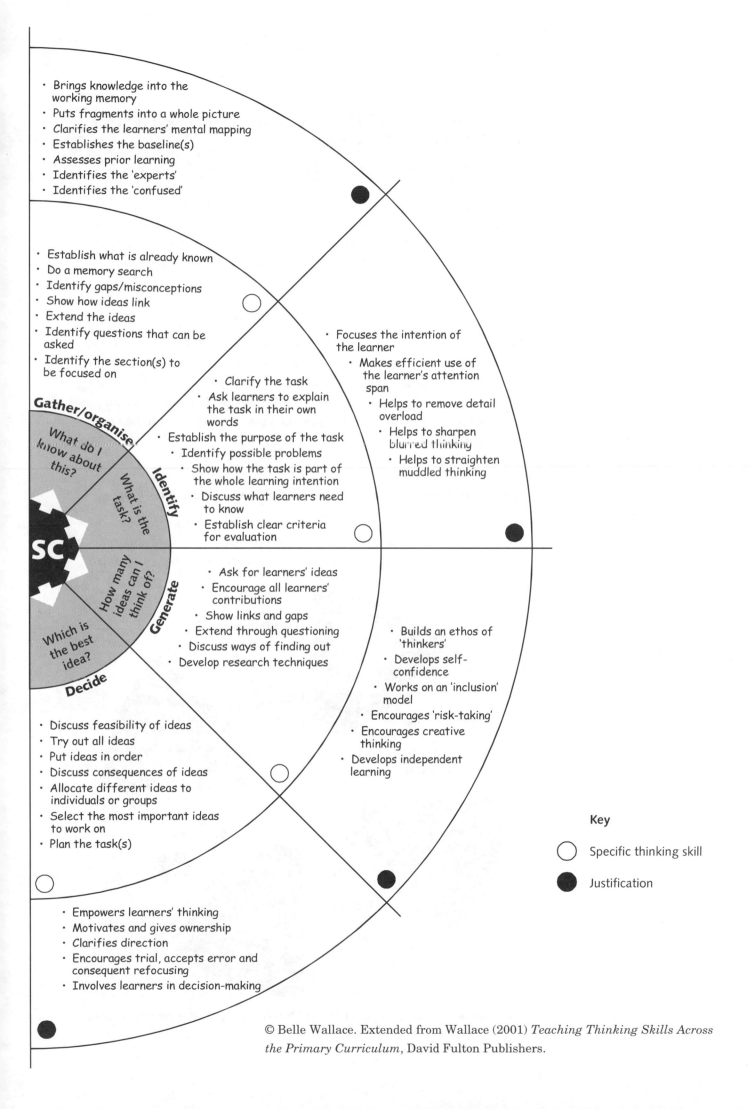

- Brings knowledge into the working memory
- Puts fragments into a whole picture
- Clarifies the learners' mental mapping
- Establishes the baseline(s)
- Assesses prior learning
- Identifies the 'experts'
- Identifies the 'confused'

- Establish what is already known
- Do a memory search
- Identify gaps/misconceptions
- Show how ideas link
- Extend the ideas
- Identify questions that can be asked
- Identify the section(s) to be focused on

- Focuses the intention of the learner
- Makes efficient use of the learner's attention span
- Helps to remove detail overload
- Helps to sharpen blurred thinking
- Helps to straighten muddled thinking

- Clarify the task
- Ask learners to explain the task in their own words
- Establish the purpose of the task
- Identify possible problems
- Show how the task is part of the whole learning intention
- Discuss what learners need to know
- Establish clear criteria for evaluation

Gather/organise

What do I know about this?

What is the task?

Identify

SC

How many ideas can I think of?

Which is the best idea?

Generate

Decide

- Ask for learners' ideas
- Encourage all learners' contributions
- Show links and gaps
- Extend through questioning
- Discuss ways of finding out
- Develop research techniques

- Builds an ethos of 'thinkers'
- Develops self-confidence
- Works on an 'inclusion' model
- Encourages 'risk-taking'
- Encourages creative thinking
- Develops independent learning

- Discuss feasibility of ideas
- Try out all ideas
- Put ideas in order
- Discuss consequences of ideas
- Allocate different ideas to individuals or groups
- Select the most important ideas to work on
- Plan the task(s)

- Empowers learners' thinking
- Motivates and gives ownership
- Clarifies direction
- Encourages trial, accepts error and consequent refocusing
- Involves learners in decision-making

Key

◯ Specific thinking skill

● Justification

© Belle Wallace. Extended from Wallace (2001) *Teaching Thinking Skills Across the Primary Curriculum*, David Fulton Publishers.

Developing Tools for Effective Thinking that feed into the TASC Problem-solving Wheel

Although there are a vast number of thinking *tools* that can feed into the TASC Problem-solving Wheel, the diagram below portrays a 'starter kit'. These core tools emerged over and over again in the original action research project which trialled and refined the TASC Model and it is worth examining these in detail. These thinking tools not only apply to effective learning but also to effective living.

Clarifying goals: What are we trying to do?

Many learners get confused with the complexity of the task and get sidetracked by irrelevant detail, often spending too much time decorating the final piece of work without being clear about the key messages they are presenting. It is essential that learners explain to each other what the actual purpose of task is; they need to be clear about their goals.

Creating a 'think-tank': How many ideas can we think of?

Often, pupils jump into the 'doing' before considering a range of possibilities. Very able learners are used to quick and easy success – 'doing the stint' without too much effort: while less able pupils are

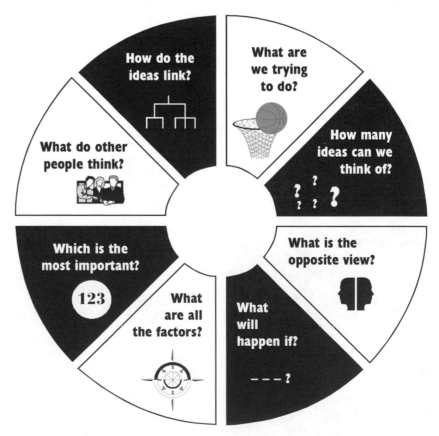

Some of the most commonly used TASC Tools for Effective Thinking (Wallace 2000)

relieved that they manage to have an idea at all! Spending a few minutes for the class to explore possibilities widens horizons and encourages creative thinking. Learners need to know that we all 'hitch-hike' on to other people's ideas and that teamwork is a good way to spark off thinking.

Looking at both sides of an idea: What is the opposite view?

Most young adolescents are egocentric and self-opinionated; stepping into someone else's shoes in any situation inevitably brings about a more balanced opinion, decision or action. Role play and discussion particularly help learners to develop a pattern of behaviour that automatically seeks the other viewpoint.

Exploring the consequences: What will happen if?

Young learners tend to be impulsive, latching on to the idea, the action or the conclusion before stopping to think of the possible consequences. The highly creative thinker can often think of another interpretation, another method or solution; we need to encourage all learners to change the accepted and the usual way of thinking and doing.

Looking all round an idea: What are all the factors to consider?

Gathering all the evidence, getting an overview and assembling all the relevant information are essential pre-planning stages. Pupils are less likely to make mistakes or to draw inadequate conclusions if they are fully prepared beforehand. They are less likely to be thrown by factors they never considered.

Prioritising: Which is the most important?

Sequencing ideas and actions in order of importance lies at the root of summarising, and the efficient accomplishment of goals. Far too many learners waffle and go round in circles, not really knowing where they are going or the most efficient way to get there.

Consulting others: What do other people think?

Most people learn best when they can share with others, exchanging knowledge, ideas, methods and experience. We are social beings and become cooperative and responsible through interaction with good group role models.

Making connections: How do the ideas link?

In school we all acquired large amounts of fragmented knowledge which we memorised, spat out and mostly forgot. Unless learners first recall what they already know, and then make meaningful links with the new knowledge, the latter soon disappears; and as teachers we usually resort to repetition and drill so that learners 'remember'. Memory works best when we can make the links, see the relevance, and use the new knowledge to solve problems. Making mindmaps of any kind helps pupils to absorb in a meaningful way and then they can more easily recall the knowledge, skills and methods as a whole learning experience.

REFLECT

Think about the core of Effective Tools for thinking outlined above:

- Which thinking tools do you use most often?

- Do you name these tools as you use them?

- Can you add more tools to your teaching repertoire?

Extending the TASC Tools for Effective Thinking

There are many action words that can be called Tools for Effective Thinking. Some of these are subject specific, while others are general and used across the curriculum. The mindmap opposite gives a comprehensive collection of cross-curricular thinking tools. The mindmap is useful as a checklist when planning classroom activities. Most of the tools are both necessary and suitable for all learners although the language would need to be adjusted to suit the level of understanding of various groups of learners.

REFLECT

- Read the mindmap opposite and check whether you consistently use the range of action words (thinking tools), and whether the words are part of the pupils' daily vocabulary.

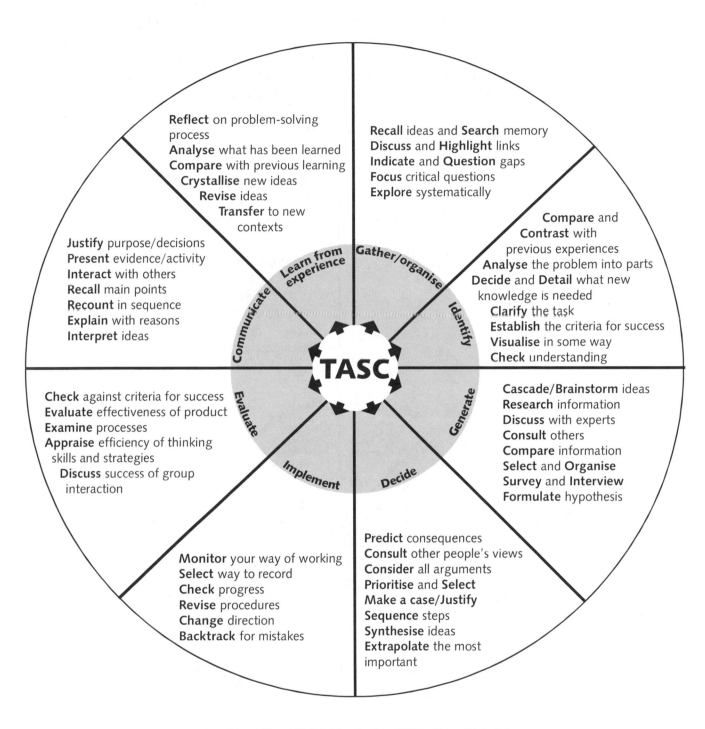

Reflect on problem-solving process
Analyse what has been learned
Compare with previous learning
Crystallise new ideas
Revise ideas
Transfer to new contexts

Recall ideas and **Search** memory
Discuss and **Highlight** links
Indicate and **Question** gaps
Focus critical questions
Explore systematically

Justify purpose/decisions
Present evidence/activity
Interact with others
Recall main points
Recount in sequence
Explain with reasons
Interpret ideas

Compare and **Contrast** with previous experiences
Analyse the problem into parts
Decide and **Detail** what new knowledge is needed
Clarify the task
Establish the criteria for success
Visualise in some way
Check understanding

Learn from experience
Gather/organise
Communicate
Identify
Evaluate
TASC
Generate
Implement
Decide

Check against criteria for success
Evaluate effectiveness of product
Examine processes
Appraise efficiency of thinking skills and strategies
Discuss success of group interaction

Cascade/Brainstorm ideas
Research information
Discuss with experts
Consult others
Compare information
Select and **Organise**
Survey and **Interview**
Formulate hypothesis

Monitor your way of working
Select way to record
Check progress
Revise procedures
Change direction
Backtrack for mistakes

Predict consequences
Consult other people's views
Consider all arguments
Prioritise and **Select**
Make a case/Justify
Sequence steps
Synthesise ideas
Extrapolate the most important

Extending the TASC Tools for Effective Thinking

Extending children's questions for thinking

All pupils need to develop a repertoire of questions to promote their thinking and which they gradually learn to use automatically. For this to happen, we need to *model* the questions as we interact in the classroom and the learners need to have a framework that they can refer to when they are working. The following mindmap provides a repertoire of questions which the pupils can keep in their 'thinking logbook' and refer to when they are working.

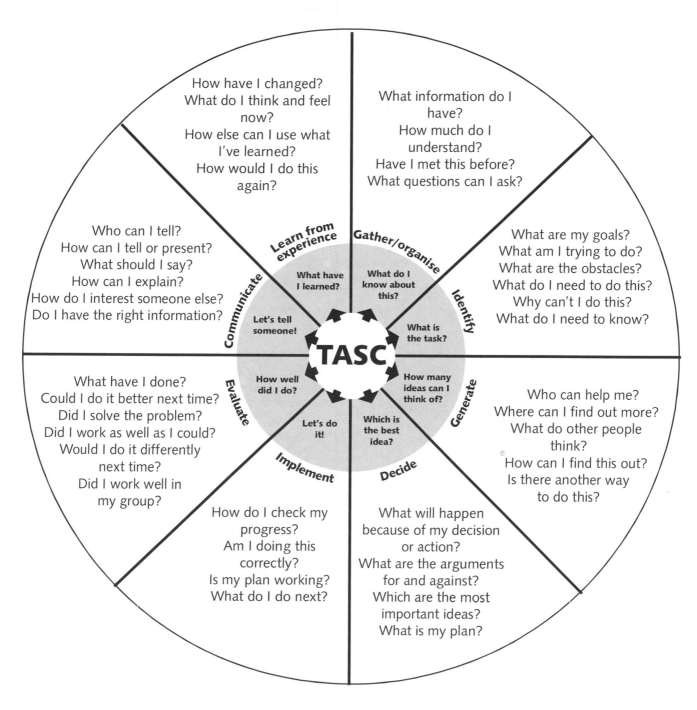

Questions to develop thinking in the TASC Problem-solving Model

● Take time to do a reflective audit of the range of questions you encourage the pupils to ask while they are working. If necessary, make a conscious effort to widen the range of questions you promote.

Conclusion: Why TASC?

A worldwide criticism of young people is that they do not *think*! And, sadly, there is an increasingly wide range of complex problems in our societies that need to be solved. It is impossible for teachers to do all the work and to solve all of society's problems, nor should they be expected to do so: parents must play their part; curriculum planners must allow teachers the freedom to teach in a thinking skills way; and adults in general need to assess what messages they convey to young people.

Nevertheless, developing learners' problem-solving and thinking skills should be an essential ingredient in the development of a humane and empowering curriculum, and there are real indications that curriculum planners realise that 'raising standards' means far more than prescribing and testing content. The National Curriculum Strategy does demand that learners learn a range of problem-solving and thinking skills, but what is not realised is that teaching and learning in this way *needs less content and more thinking time.* The development of thinking skills is not a matter of 'add-on' exercises but a holistic approach to the whole curriculum.

However, as teachers we also need to realise that spending time on developing learners' thinking skills makes them more efficient learners and when the pupils have a repertoire of effective problem-solving and thinking skills, *we save time because the children are better able to learn.*

We all learn best when we:

● understand and can see the relevance of what we are learning;

● can relate to our cultural context;

● can appreciate the purpose of the tasks that are set;

● can fit the fragments into the whole picture;

● have experiences of real success;

● use what we know to develop more complex mental schemes;

● can hook into new knowledge from the base we already have;

● acquire new techniques and thinking skills through modelling and demonstration;

● practise skills that lead to confidence and competence.

When the thinking skills tide comes in all ships rise!

In the following chapters, we look at TASC in action with teachers and pupils.

- In Chapter 2, Richard Bentley and Elizabeth Johnstone describe a programme that focuses on the introduction of TASC based problem-solving skills through a non-curricular approach.
- Nigel Kent explores a particular angle on famine relief in Chapter 3, which focuses on literacy, combining TASC problem-solving skills with the development of essential writing and multi-media skills.
- Chapter 4, written by Jeanette Brocks, Melisa Bayliss and Sue Foster-Agg, uses the TASC model as a framework for problem-solving activities in the development of skills in numeracy.
- Rashu Rosso and Lucy Bell-Scott work with groups of pupils to combine the TASC model with specific skills in science problem-solving, developing these in Chapter 5 as an extension of the Tools for Effective Thinking in Science.
- Chapter 6, written by Jane Finch, records how a 'local crime' can be solved by using the TASC principles combined with ICT.

Getting the Wheels Turning:

Putting TASC into Action

RICHARD BENTLEY and ELIZABETH JOHNSTONE

Although it may seem self-evident, focusing on thinking skills in the classroom is important because it supports active cognitive processing which makes for better learning . . . many writers argue that setting standards is not sufficient for raising standards. Standards can only be raised when attention is directed not only to what is to be learned but on how children learn and how teachers intervene to achieve this . . .

(McGuiness 1999)

REFLECT

The opening chapter, then, has explored the TASC paradigm and the rationale behind it. Let's assume that, like us, you have been struck by the clarity of TASC, and appreciate its potential relevance in terms of supporting students and teachers alike in developing the problem-solving process, and in supporting schools as they develop and refine 'the thinking classroom' and an overall thinking climate.

How do you introduce TASC to a group of students, a class, a year group, a school or a group of teachers? What is an effective way of getting started?

PURPOSE

In our LEA advisory role we have been involved in supporting the introduction of TASC to a number of primary, middle and secondary schools. In this chapter we outline an 'introductory programme' that we have developed, with Belle Wallace's help and support, and which has proved effective for students and teachers in Key Stages 2 and 3. We use the TASC model itself (and the TASC icons) as the basis for describing, justifying and evaluating this programme of activities.

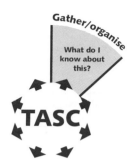

What do we know already about thinking skills and problem-solving?

We have gathered information and research evidence that confirm the significance of thinking and problem-solving skills as a central aspect of teaching and learning, and that:

● improvement in the development of thinking and problem-solving skills will reflect positively in standards overall;

● it is possible to support all students in developing their thinking and problem-solving skills, and improving the use of these skills;

● such support depends upon the provision of structured and balanced opportunities to practise and develop skills (including reflection and transfer skills), and upon an appropriate climate;

● group work, role play and other collaborative experiences form important social and communicative aspects of the development of thinking and problem-solving skills; and

● TASC is an ideal vehicle for supporting the provision and uptake of this blend of cognitive and social learning opportunities.

At the same time, we have seen schools develop their use of TASC in a number of ways, but usually via one of two routes; both routes can be effective, but both have associated pitfalls.

Route A *The contagious route*

Once introduced (probably by an individual teacher), use of the TASC model spreads through a school as colleagues become increasingly aware of, and curious about, the approach; staff are involved, largely haphazardly, by personal contact.

Of course:

● it may *not* spread naturally, and 'stick' due to local circumstances or misconceptions;

● important messages (and even principles) may be lost, confused or diluted;

● people meeting TASC second or third hand may not have a full enough understanding of the paradigm/may not realise the power and place of TASC.

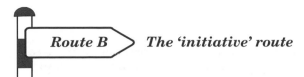

Route B ▷ *The 'initiative' route*

A head teacher or teacher attempts to introduce TASC across a whole school (or perhaps Key Stage) on a more structured basis; staff are involved as a group.

Of course:

- individual staff may not be ready (or even willing) to focus on thinking skills/TASC;

- some teachers may see it as additional work – another initiative – rather than a central aspect of teaching and learning;

- it may be seen as an academic (and largely irrelevant) model, its practical opportunities and potential, and the usefulness to students and teachers alike, not being recognised.

In relation to both routes:

- teachers may accept the model, but not the specific relevance to their own situation (subject, curriculum, classroom);

- teachers may underestimate pupil involvement with, and enjoyment and understanding of, TASC.

The aim – and hopefully the end-product – of both routes is the same. It is the emergence and refinement of a shared whole-school approach to problem-solving and thinking skills development; the planning and provision of structured curricular (and extra-curricular) opportunities for problem-solving, offered within an appropriate thinking climate.

And TASC is the basis for this development, ensuring well-grounded structure, balance of coverage and confidence to both pupils and teachers alike.

We believe that both routes – and variations of them – can be supported by the inclusion of an introductory or familiarisation 'package' of experiences that serve to introduce TASC to pupils (and staff).

Are you able to identify yourself or your school within either 'route'?

Have you an interest in introducing a class/year group/Key Stage/ subject team/school to a more structured approach to the development of thinking and problem-solving skills?

If so, read on.

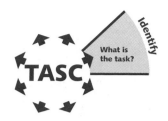

What did we set out to do?

We set out to devise, plan and carry out a programme of introductory activities that would support both routes and which would:

● introduce pupils to the TASC model and its rationale, and enable them to apply a basic understanding of the problem-solving process to a range of problem contexts;

● be fast (we set ourselves a two-day limit to the introductory programme), flexible and fun;

● have an in-service training potential as well as being useful to the pupils involved – that is, we wanted teachers taking part to also increase their understanding of, and confidence in, TASC;

● form a basic 'introductory' package – or series of related and progressive tasks – that teachers/schools could build on and personalise to their own professional circumstances;

● model an approach to be developed into a range of curricular experiences, and embedded as problem-solving strategy.

The following mindmap develops this thinking.

FAST

Can be carried over a two-day period. This could be longer, but as curriculum time is so short we set ourselves a two-day limit. This could be extended, and we suggest directions for extension

FLEXIBLE

• Has relevance to both routes, is cross-curricular (subject free), but has obvious application to a range of curricular areas. • Is suitable for pupils with a range of abilities • Emphasises the social (collaborative) and group aspect of TASC • Emphasises communication – language as a means of developing higher order thinking skills • Is suitable for the middle years (KS2 and KS3 age range) – we tried it with mixed age groups and single year groups in a 9–13 middle school • Could be used with a whole school or Key Stage, but also had relevance in a single class or group • Could be used at any point in the school year, beginning or summer term, perhaps as part of a transition and transfer programme

FUN

Not too serious. Allows students to relax and focus on thinking processes (i.e. metacognition)

We wanted the introductory programme to have an in-service training potential as well as being useful to the pupils involved (that is, we wanted teachers taking part to also increase their understanding of, and confidence in, TASC) and to produce material, including an exemplar introductory programme, which we could offer to interested teachers, head teachers and schools.

We wanted a basic introductory package, or series of related and progressive tasks, which teachers/schools could build on and personalise.

We also wanted to model an approach to be developed and subsequently transferred into a range of curricular areas.

At the end of the two-day introductory/familiarisation programme:

We wanted teachers to say . . .   *And so demonstrate . . .*

Yes, but that's only good teaching and learning . . .

awareness of the central role/place of thinking skills/problem-solving in teaching and learning

I have a better feel for a thinking classroom

a better appreciation of the features/characteristics of a thinking climate

That's really relevant to my subject/class/curriculum/ school . . .

personalisation of model to professional situation

I'm going to try that . . . I can see how it would help me to get more out of my pupils

enthusiasm to adopt, understanding of relevance to curriculum, and to raising standards across the board

I have a better understanding of the way different students approach problem-solving tasks

appreciation of different learning styles and related learning needs

I see now how working in groups can help children to develop thinking and problem-solving skills

appreciation of genuinely collaborative work, i.e. working in groups rather than simply being arranged in groups

Now I can see how I can help students to think better

clearer understanding of intervention and support strategies ––when and how to intervene – and why

I feel more confident in using TASC terminology – it's coming naturally

ability to model appropriate thinking and problem-solving language

We wanted students to say . . .   *And so demonstrate . . .*

That was really good fun – I enjoyed that . . .

enjoyment of learning

That has helped to make me a better problem solver . . .

understanding and internalisation of the model

 I can use TASC in all sorts of situations and all sorts of subjects . . .

an appreciation and awareness of transfer potential

 Now I understand more about how I think

increased metacognitive awareness

Now I appreciate better the value of working in a team . . .

greater awareness of social context and its potential advantages

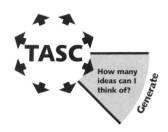

So we put our heads together and came up with all sorts of ideas – some of them a bit vague at first, and some of them perhaps unlikely to work – but the important thing (as reinforced in TASC itself) is to consider all possibilities.

Ideas thrown up in this process may be broadly divided into **organisational** opportunities and **content** opportunities, as shown below.

Organisational opportunities	Content opportunities
We need students working in groups	Justify decisions
Working in different size groups	Experience the need to compromise
Bring groups together as larger groups	Give different presentations
Let's include something that gets them to see how we can put ideas together and have a bigger idea pool . . . focus on thinking	Experience role play
	Different sorts of problems – including real problems
We need to ask them if they understand how they think	Open-ended tasks
Do they know what sort of thinkers they are?	Limits to solution – and keep them tight/be strict
We need to get them to brainstorm possibilities	Stay curriculum-neutral at this stage – no obvious subject links or labels
	Have a broad theme
conservation? sustainability?	Focus on the Wheel as a whole and on individual segments in early stages, then bring together

Using these mindmaps and resulting criteria, we devised a series of free-standing but sequential activities to familiarise students (and teachers) with TASC. The initial activities focused on skills within the first half of the TASC Wheel, stopping short of 'implementing'. Then two longer activities embraced all the skills within the Wheel, including provision of opportunities for experience in implementation and post-implementation skills (that is, the second half of the Wheel).

Detailed plans of the activities are provided as a photocopiable resource on the following pages.

Activities	Particularly looking for
DAY 1 **Morning** 1 Memory search: The brain	Gather/Organise
2 Using your bottle	Gather/Organise, Generate, Decide
3 Preparing for a day's trek …	Gather/Organise, Identify, Generate, Decide
Afternoon 4 Saving the Erar	TASC
DAY 2 5 The Persuaders	TASC

DAY ONE

ACTIVITY I

Memory search: The Brain

Let's gather together everything we know about 'the brain'.
Let's get all our 'bits and pieces of information' together.

Work in groups of four for a few minutes, giving each group a chance to think. Then take feedback from the whole group. Record on an A1 sheet or flipchart. Use a second colour and ask the children which bits of information link together and draw link lines.

This activity is intended to help students to see that:

- in addressing any problem an efficient starting point is to pull together any information/ ideas (the starting point for mindmapping);

- the sum of collective knowledge in the group is greater than that of any individual (and so the group is a useful source of information and ideas in solving a problem);

- it is possible to improve performance through practising such activities so we can 'train the brain'.

 Note particularly

- The potential for revising and reorganising after 'first-thoughting' and the collection of ideas.

- The potential for 'hitch-hiking' on other people's ideas (this may be a particularly useful strategy for less confident pupils).

TASC focus: Gather/ Organise

Modelling focus: how to organise, classify and group responses

DAY ONE

ACTIVITY 2

Using your bottle

How many uses can you think of for a plastic bottle?

Start in groups of four with one 2-litre plastic bottle per group. Brainstorm/first-thought ideas and write them down. (Ideas can be as unusual as students wish.) Ask each group to prioritise their three 'best' ideas. Then bring groups together into larger groups (perhaps one large group). Have each group offer their top idea, then their second idea, and then the third. List the ideas on the flipchart – emphasise no repeats.

This activity is intended to:

- alert teachers to pupils' potential for creative thinking;

- help pupils to become more confident in offering, and building on, suggestions.

 Note particularly

- Some pupils will reuse the bottle as another container, some will change its purpose but use the basic shape (for example as a skittle), some will change the shape (for example suggesting cutting or melting it), some will add to the bottle (for example fins to make a space shuttle).

- To help students to further practise the skills introduced in Activity 1 and to help pupils to think in different ways and to be confident in offering unusual ideas (so moving closer towards establishing a 'risk-taking' climate).

TASC focus: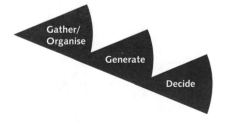

Modelling focus: discuss
listen
prioritise
justify prioritisation
think creatively

DAY ONE

ACTIVITY 3

Preparing for a day's trek through the hills/jungle/desert/rainforest

Identify a list of the things you need to take with you on the trek.

Divide the students into groups of four and ask them to brainstorm what they already know about trekking through the hills / jungle / desert / rainforest. Clarify the task (considering all factors). Ask them to generate a list of all the things they need to take with them. Then ask them to decide on the five most important things they must have (prioritising) and why they need them (justifying).

This activity is intended to help students to:

● repeat and further practise the intended outcomes of Activities 1 and 2;

● emphasise clarification of the task (looking around the task at all possibilities);

● experience being projected into different and future situations (role play and empathy).

TASC focus: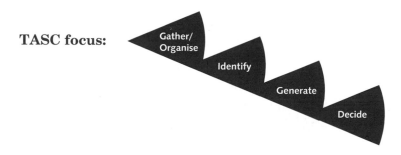

Modelling focus: decide
                       justify
                       generate

Activities 1, 2 and 3 have drawn attention to and practised specific segments of the TASC Wheel in preparation for Activities 4 and 5, which set out to bring the full Wheel into play (with differing emphases).

DAY ONE

ACTIVITY 4

Saving the Erar

Build a free-standing structure (as tall as possible) to transport an Erar egg to the ground as slowly as possible.

With this activity give the students the following information to contextualise the problem:

The Erar is a very unusual and rare bird, which builds its nest on the ground. That sounds OK, but on this occasion it hasn't laid its single egg in the nest but has chosen, instead, to lay it on the branches of a tree. To save this bird from extinction the students need to build something to transport an Erar egg carefully from the branch to the ground.

The students should work in groups of four or five (the key issue is to change both size and composition of the groups from the previous day). One set of the following equipment is to be made available to each group, and nothing else is to be used:

- *2 sheets of card (A1 size)*
- *8 large paper clips*
- *8 art straws*
- *4 sheets of scrap paper (A4) for planning*

- *a ping-pong ball / plastic egg*
- *4 strong elastic bands*
- *2 half-metre strips of Sellotape*
- *2 pairs of scissors*

Each group should also have access to a stop-watch (for trialling / presentation).

This activity is intended to help students to:

- bring together skills previously practised but within a different group setting (familiar skills but unfamiliar group);

- extend work through the whole TASC Wheel (and so experience the whole Wheel in operation);

- focus on the second half of the Wheel and so meet new skills in the areas of implementation, evaluation, communication and learning from experience;

- tackle a 'real' (if far-fetched) problem (and so put skills into a real problem-solving context);

- introduce, through evaluation, the notion of different criteria and issues of measurement (getting students to agree on measures and measuring strategies);

- practise interpretation of deliberately limited instructions/data provided, and to make own decisions on detail.

Note particularly

- Planning – tendency for students to rush into action without planning.

- Guidance level/detail – tendency for students to ask for very specific guidance; the need sometimes to break the culture of always 'asking the teacher'.

TASC focus:

Modelling focus: using empowering language, for example:

    'You decide . . .'
    'No right answer . . .'
    'What do you think?'
    'That's up to your group to decide . . .'
    'Why did you decide to . . .?'

DAY TWO

LINK ACTIVITY TO BEGIN DAY TWO

As a whole group run round the TASC Wheel!

What did we learn from yesterday, about ourselves as thinkers and about problem-solving?

Focus on the different vocabulary associated with each segment (modelled vocabulary). Different questions are helpful in exploring each segment. We used the version of the Wheel on page 22 for this.

Just before starting Activity 5 tell students that this activity really will test their expertise in using the TASC Wheel but at the same time emphasise that the Wheel will see them successfully through it (stressing the supportive nature of the Wheel).

DAY TWO

ACTIVITY 5

The Persuaders (Selling your idea)

Thinking-up, designing and selling a game.

Today is about looking at the potential power of a family game to communicate a 'message'. Later we'll outline the specific task, which involves thinking-up, designing and selling a game. First, let's look at some games and assess their qualities.

Stage 1: Look at – and play – a selection of board games

Look at issues like:

● Does it have a specific setting?

● What type of game is it?

● Who is it designed to be played by?

● What skills are required of the players? (Are these appropriate for the age range specified?)

● To what extent does it depend on chance?

● Does it look attractive?

● Would you buy it? What in particular attracts you or puts you off?

● Who might purchase it? (Parents, children, relatives, schools?)

Do not give the students the above criteria but elicit as much as possible from them, topping up if necessary. As they play, encourage students to take on one of the age group roles within the range specified on the game.

Stage 2: Devise a game of your own

The activity is to decide, in groups of three or four, on a design for a board or other family game that is a potential 'best seller'. By the afternoon, the students should aim to be in a position to present, and justify, their design to a panel representing a company that manufactures games.

The game has to:

● *convey a social message (the example we used was a message relating to an aspect of conservation).;*

● *be appropriate for a range of family members / age groups;*

● *be usable in a family context and so not be a computer game;*

● *be potentially marketable world-wide.*

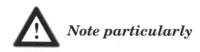 *Note particularly*

The emphasis must be on *ideas*, and not on actually *making* the game (to avoid the danger of time being misused colouring in a board).

Join each group to another one or two groups (organise combined groups of eight or nine).

Stage 3: Select one design to be put forward to the manufacturing company's panel in the afternoon, and prepare the presentation

To do this, each group will have to explain details of their original game to the other group. Then discussion will lead to a composite design.

Don't take one idea only and abandon the other idea(s). We hope to see features/aspects of all the games in the final game plan. And we shall later be interested in hearing which aspects were incorporated, and why.

Everyone in the group has to have a role in the presentation and its preparation (the roles will vary).

Stage 4: Prepare a ten-minute presentation of your game (on the four acetate sheets) for this afternoon's meeting with the game manufacturer's panel

You have one hour in which to do this. The whole group will be going to the meeting and will need to introduce themselves and briefly state their contribution to the final game. You will need to decide who is presenting on behalf of the group although all of you will need to be prepared to answer questions.

Present your ideas in any way you wish, but you might like to consider:

- *designing the box/packaging and the rules of the game;*
- *putting together a story-board of a television advertisement (for which you need to present all the key information in a short time, so you should decide what would appear on screen and in the voiceover);*
- *designing a poster advertising your game.*

Remember that the presentation will be limited to 7–10 minutes, so stress that the students need to keep to key points.

Stage 5: The presentation

Each group presents to the panel in turn. Panel roles can be, for example, design/marketing director, finance director, parent/family consultant. In addition to a family consultant, some firms use children in a similar role so all those students not involved in the presentation assume this 'child adviser' role, and score games (as presented) against the previously agreed criteria.

Panel follows by asking some presentation-specific questions/clarification. Students justify/expand points in role as designers. The panel gives feedback and so models evaluation against criteria.

© Belle Wallace (2002) *Teaching Thinking Skills Across the Middle Years*, David Fulton Publishers.

'The Persuaders' activity (Stages 1–5) is intended to help students to see:

- that the first idea may not be the best idea – they should be prepared to continue exploration of ideas, and be prepared to jettison ideas;

- that to achieve the task they need to work genuinely collaboratively, and to take the ideas of others on board;

- the importance of communicating ideas succinctly and being able to justify their group's decisions;

- the advantages of role play (seeing things through the eyes of another person) and of presenting, in role, to a 'real' audience;

- the importance of evaluation, and different ways of making judgements;

- the importance of revisiting and improving following evaluation.

TASC focus

Modelling focus

Both the TASC focus and the modelling focus vary and develop between the different stages of the activity but, overall, Activity 5 focuses on the whole TASC Wheel and related modelling vocabulary.

So that's what we did, but all the time keeping in mind certain 'rules to encourage thinking'. We kept reminding ourselves to:

- Keep flexible (for example, in terms of timings and groupings) in order to respond to the developing situation and student responses.

> This is going really well, but we can see some of you need a bit longer. We'll give you another 7 minutes on this.

- Keep pushing and demanding – maintaining appropriately high expectations and not letting complacency creep into the responses.

> This is very good, but I'm sure this group can come up with some even more unusual ideas for this.

- Keep intervention to a minimum – but where necessary keeping focused and always encouraging the student to provide the answer (or, at least, the next step forward).

> Well, what do *you* think . . .?
> *Why* do you think . . .?

- Keep intended outcomes firmly in sight.

> What is the purpose of this?
> What are you trying to do?

- Not let tasks be taken over by a few – trying to maintain genuine involvement for all group members.

> Is everyone having a say?
> Are you using all the members of your group effectively?

- Make good (and easily retrievable) notes of inset points – including potentially significant student observations and responses.

> Excellent metacognition going on here.
> Note the group interaction here.

- Support transfer.

> Have you come across this sort of task before? How have you used that word before? Does this remind you of any problem you've had to solve before?

- Support metacognitive reflection – helping students to think aloud.

> That's interesting! Just explain to me why you decided to tackle it that way. What was your plan when you decided to . . .? What were the reasons behind that?

● Recognise success.

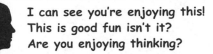

That's good thinking!
That's good organisation!
Keep on exploring the issue!

● Keep it fun.

I can see you're enjoying this!
This is good fun isn't it?
Are you enjoying thinking?

In other words, we were very much focusing on maintaining – and all the time further developing – an appropriate 'thinking climate'.

To what extent do you think these 'rules to encourage thinking' will support the development of a thinking climate?

Are there 'rules' that you would want to challenge? Or qualify? Or add?

So did our introductory programme achieve what it set out to achieve?

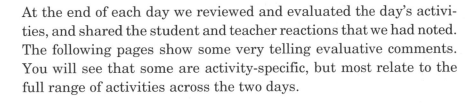

● Was it fast, flexible and fun?

● Did it introduce students to the TASC model and its rationale, and provide them with a basic understanding of thinking and problem-solving processes that they might take forwards – with TASC – to a range of problem and curricular contexts?

● Did it additionally contain a useful element of in-service training/continuing professional development?

At the end of each day we reviewed and evaluated the day's activities, and shared the student and teacher reactions that we had noted. The following pages show some very telling evaluative comments. You will see that some are activity-specific, but most relate to the full range of activities across the two days.

Teachers' Comments

I found it non-threatening being in a cross-curricular context.

Being cross-curricular helped me to spot and think about key issues more easily.

I think it will help me to balance the work I do on thinking skills.

It will help my planning.

I was surprised at the overall quality of some of the pupil reactions.

I can now see the opportunity for a maths version of the Wheel. [One is included in Chapter 4.]

It was interesting to see the pupils operating in different learning groups.

I was surprised because some of the best responses were from unexpected sources.

I was amazed at how often they referred to the TASC model and consulted their badges. [All the students wore a name badge that included the TASC Wheel.]

Didn't they enjoy it!

I was surprised at how willing they were to challenge the Wheel and to try to improve it.

The groups approached the activities in different ways – some of them just rushed into making without any planning discussion.

I really enjoyed working this way with the children.

They offered some really good additional questions to add to the Wheel.

Students' Comments

It's good how you can use it in lots of different ways.

This justifying is a bit like justifying in science.

I think I'm good at making lots of suggestions - this is a good activity for me.

I really enjoyed that.

This is so frustrating.

Aren't you going to tell us how to do it?

Can you go backwards in the Wheel? – We need to change the decision because it's not working.

When you have to decide on your 'best' solution, how do you know it is really the best?

Our best idea will take too long, so we're going to abandon it and go for another.

Presenting to the panel was just like acting on a stage.

Can you change the shape of the bottle – like melt it? Can you cut it? Can you add bits on?

Our group is really good at coming up with lots of ideas.

We're not so good at prioritising.

Working this way means you really have to think . . . it was easier when the teacher gave you more help.

I like listening to other people's ideas, it helps me come up with better ideas of my own.

Having to explain my ideas to others and then listening to their ideas helps *my* thinking.

REFLECT

To what extent do the two sets of observations reflect shared perceptions and understanding?

What are the implications for learning? And what are the implications for planning and teaching?

To what extent do these teacher and student observations reflect features of a thinking climate?

So now we have material to offer to schools as a set of introductory activities to TASC. But we see it as much more than that. The introductory activity is the first stage of a longer process. Indeed, what we have set out is the first two days of what we hope will be the way that the students and teachers involved will work for the rest of their lives!

So, how do we go about spreading the word?

Well, through in-service training, of course. There are a number of ways in which we propose to develop thinking-skills initiatives. One is by using the same introductory activities with teachers, supported by appropriate thinking-skills background and theory; they then take the package back to school and lead it (having experienced it themselves), with us maintaining support (particularly in the areas of analysis and evaluation).

And wider dissemination is also via this chapter! What you are reading is part of the communication segment of the TASC Wheel.

We hope, too, that dissemination will bring further reaction and comment, and so opportunities to *revisit* the evaluation segment and other segments of the TASC Wheel.

The introductory programme we have outlined has been used with students in Year 6 of primary schools, Years 7 and 8 of secondary schools and Years 6, 7 and 8 of middle schools. In all these middle years contexts, it has been seen to be an effective and non-threatening way into TASC. It has proved itself to be a powerful teaching and learning experience for pupils and teachers.

There are, of course, other ways of introducing TASC. The overall plan, timetabling, and the activities themselves could be different. It is very important that the detail of the introduction suits both the school and the key staff involved. It needs to be personalised in presentation terms to the school's own setting and situation. 'Presenters' need to be comfortable with it, but not so comfortable that they don't take risks!

Whatever the content and pattern of the introduction, the principles we have set out in this chapter remain applicable. Use them to test any variation of an introductory programme that you may devise.

Principles checklist (for introductory activities)

☐ Cross-curricular (but able to lead into a range of subject-based curriculum activities)

☐ Appropriate for all abilities

☐ Explores and practises individual segments of TASC as well as whole Wheel

☐ Utilises different groups and ways of collaborative working (and so emphasise the 'social context' aspect of the problem-solving model)

☐ Models appropriate problem-solving language and strategies

☐ Guarantees a significant degree of success, and so helps to build and boost student confidence in problem-solving strategies (and group work)

☐ Both reflects and further develops a thinking climate

☐ Helps to support teachers' understanding of thinking-skills development, and makes a contribution to their continuing professional development

☐ Enjoyable (for students and teachers)

☐ Capable of being 'personalised' to the particular school/group context

So where next?

▶ REFLECT

How is this introductory package developed into a curricular context? ... and a way of working? ... and an approach to learning?

◀ COMMENT

If it were a three-day introduction, our third day (which might be a little while after the first two) would focus on a real 'school-based' problem, or a problem outside the school but one that is still very much part of the children's consciousness – either because it is local, or through television/newspaper exposure.

Examples of school-based problems might be reviewing school rules, or designing a new playground layout, or organising a summer fair. Some problems of this sort, as part of an introduction to TASC, are explored by Diana Cave in *Teaching Thinking Skills Across the Primary Curriculum* (Wallace 2001).

A 'real' local problem might involve plans for redeveloping a park or shopping precinct, or the case for a local leisure centre. Or solving a local crime (the sort of activity outlined by Jane Finch in Chapter 6). An issue further afield might involve a famine relief operation; or planning support following an earthquake.

Nigel Kent explores a particular angle on famine relief in Chapter 3, which focuses on literacy.

This leads us to consider the next and vitally important stage of the introduction of the TASC paradigm: *the subsequent development of thinking and problem-solving skills in specific curricular areas – and the adaptation of the model to support different curricular approaches.* This is what the remainder of this book sets out to explore. (Chapter 4, for example, includes the use of a 'mathematical version' of the Wheel.)

The areas under consideration are literacy, numeracy, science and ICT (the 'extended core'). However, the TASC principles will be equally applicable – and equally effective – in all curriculum areas.

Thinking Through a Literacy Project

NIGEL KENT

Although our perceptions seem to overlap, our expressions, representations, and descriptions don't. Therein lies one of the biggest barriers to communication: the lack of a common language or way of understanding one another and bridging our individual worlds . . .

Metaphorming works by helping people see the similarities among our perceptions rather than dwell on the differences of our expressions and representations. The team pilots the metaphorming process, defying the common wisdom that there can be only one pilot. All the team members begin to think as 'one for all and all for one' – without losing their voices, ideas, and diversity. They discover the real meaning and value behind the abstract expression of 'unity in diversity'. They also learn to recognise the deep rewards in integrating cross-functional ideas.　　　　(Siler 1999)

REFLECT

Take a few minutes to reflect upon the key messages about the teaching of writing that have emerged over the past 20 years and you might come up with some variation of the approaches shown overleaf.

	Process approach	Generic approach
Teachers should	● provide a range of authentic contexts for writing with real audiences and purposes – e.g. write a picture book for a child in a local feeder school ● teach explicitly how to: – brainstorm before writing – draft ideas – revise them – edit – proofread – publish.	● provide opportunities for pupils to analyse and write a range of models of different text types – narrative, persuasive, discursive, procedural etc. ● teach explicitly: – the organisational features of texts – e.g. persuasive texts have a non-linear structure – language features of texts – e.g. persuasive texts feature generalised rather than specific subjects – 'Teachers' rather than 'Mr Brown' – the grammatical features of texts – e.g. persuasive texts are generally written in the present tense.
Apprentice writers will	● collaborate with others to refine their ideas and their expression ● deploy an implicit knowledge of language acquired from previous reading and writing experiences.	● test the effectiveness of their writing by referring back to the model ● consciously apply the knowledge of texts acquired from the pre-writing analysis of models.

COMMENT ▶   Confusing, isn't it?

At the heart of these two pedagogical models lie significantly different views of apprentice writers. On the one hand, they are seen as requiring support chiefly in terms of motivation and in understanding the needs of the reader; on the other hand, they are seen as lacking the language resources and textual knowledge to communicate effectively. Consequently, it might be argued that these models serve two different groups of apprentice writers with distinct needs. The fact that all of us can recognise both types of need in our classrooms suggests that if our practice inclines towards one model, we may well be empowering one group of writers at the expense of the other. Clearly, we need classroom practice that synthesises these two pedagogical models into a single coherent approach – an approach that addresses the needs of *all* of the following pupils.

She's got lots of ideas but she can never get started.

He hates writing: he just can't see the point.

His writing just doesn't flow. His essay reads like a list of points.

She has a lovely imagination but all her stories sound the same.

She 's okay when she's writing stories but she has real difficulty organising her ideas in other sorts of writing.

His stories have brilliant openings but they run out of steam.

She can be really adventurous in her choice of language but it doesn't always come off.

Her redrafts are no more than neat copies of her first draft.

His writing lacks development.

She writes as she speaks.

Of course, unless she reads more she will never improve at writing.

I try to discuss his writing with him, but we don't seem to have the right language to be able to do so.

When I ask him to write he tells me his mind goes blank.

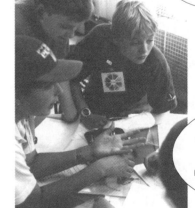
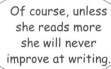

At the heart of this approach will be activities that enable apprentice writers to develop a range of distinct types of knowledge and understanding that lie at the heart of effective writing.

PURPOSE   The purpose of this chapter is to present a case study that demonstrates how the TASC Wheel has been used with apprentice writers to produce a coherent approach to the teaching of writing that synthesises the most powerful features of the process and generic approaches.

Using the TASC problem-solving and thinking-skills model helps pupils to understand themselves as writers and helps them to move towards a state of conscious competence. The TASC Wheel was used to create coherent writing opportunities for pupils in the middle years, synthesising into an effective approach the key features of the process and generic models of the teaching of writing.

The Wheel was adjusted to suit the goal of the project, while maintaining the essential elements in the TASC paradigm. Figure 1 (pages 52–3) outlines the overall framework within which we worked.

Using the TASC Wheel to support the production of a multi-media text

Relief Campaign Simulation

The following learning opportunity was undertaken by a mixed age group of children drawn from Years 6, 7 and 8 as part of an LEA summer school for more able pupils. The whole LEA summer school was built around a series of thinking and problem-solving activities. The children were introduced to the TASC Wheel and were constantly challenged to use it to guide their approach to these activities and to reflect upon their learning.

The purpose of the activity described below was to provide an opportunity to trial materials and approaches that aimed to:

- develop the skills necessary to produce an effective multi-media persuasive text;

- develop thinking and problem-solving skills by producing a campaign strategy that uses this text – they would need to decide upon their target audience and how to reach the maximum number of their target audience;

- explore the issue of representation of people in the developing world – they would need to evaluate their final product in terms of the degree to which the final version of their text maintains the dignity of the people featured within the text and avoids stereotyping; and

- develop collaborative and interpersonal skills.

For this chapter, however, I intend to focus on the first aim, in which the TASC Wheel was used to synthesise the most effective features of the process and generic approaches to the teaching of writing skills. It must be noted, however, that while the summer school provided the opportunity for a three-hour period of sustained writing, it did not provide us with unlimited access to the children. Consequently, some of the processes described below were truncated in the interests of completion of the task.

In addition to using the TASC Wheel as a thinking framework to guide the writing process, we infused the whole activity with the following questions which we challenged the students to consider and respond to.

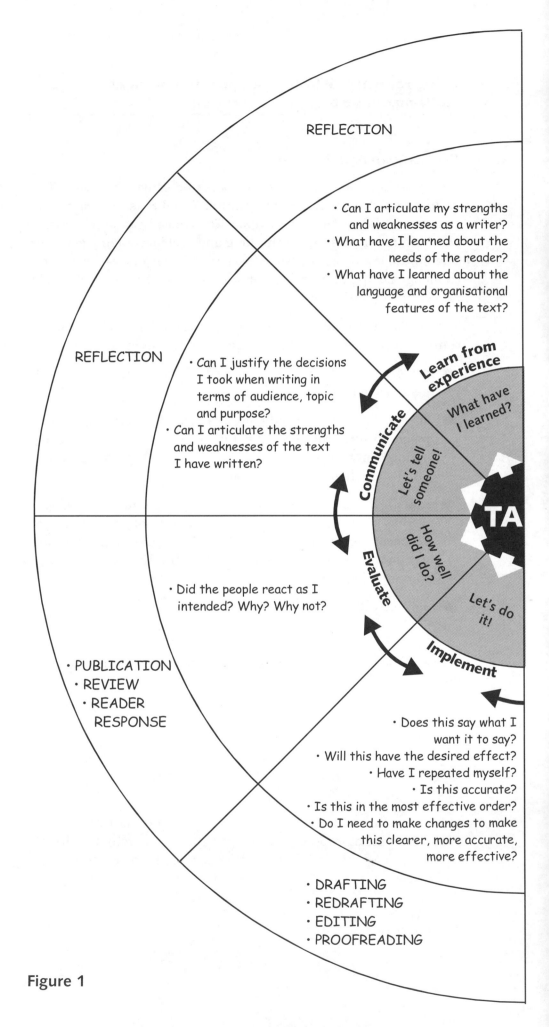

REFLECTION

REFLECTION

• Can I articulate my strengths and weaknesses as a writer?
• What have I learned about the needs of the reader?
• What have I learned about the language and organisational features of the text?

Learn from experience

What have I learned?

Communicate

Let's tell someone!

• Can I justify the decisions I took when writing in terms of audience, topic and purpose?
• Can I articulate the strengths and weaknesses of the text I have written?

How well did I do?

TA

Let's do it!

Evaluate

• Did the people react as I intended? Why? Why not?

Implement

• PUBLICATION
• REVIEW
• READER RESPONSE

• Does this say what I want it to say?
• Will this have the desired effect?
• Have I repeated myself?
• Is this accurate?
• Is this in the most effective order?
• Do I need to make changes to make this clearer, more accurate, more effective?

• DRAFTING
• REDRAFTING
• EDITING
• PROOFREADING

Figure 1

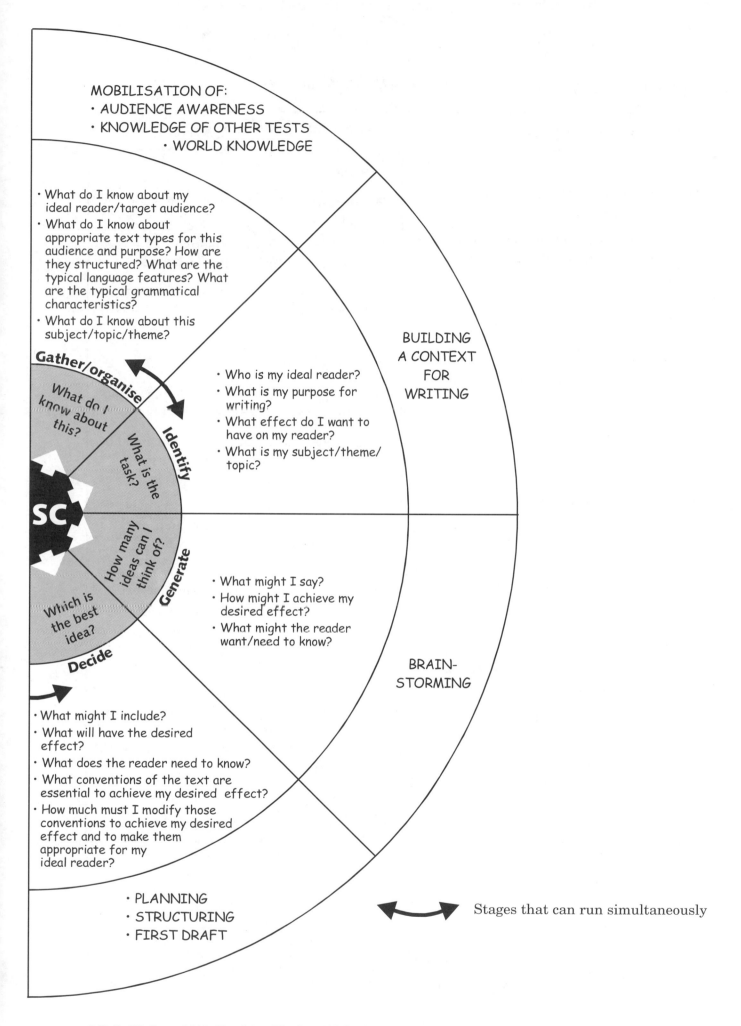

MOBILISATION OF:
• AUDIENCE AWARENESS
• KNOWLEDGE OF OTHER TESTS
• WORLD KNOWLEDGE

• What do I know about my ideal reader/target audience?
• What do I know about appropriate text types for this audience and purpose? How are they structured? What are the typical language features? What are the typical grammatical characteristics?
• What do I know about this subject/topic/theme?

BUILDING A CONTEXT FOR WRITING

Gather/organise

What do I know about this?

What is the task?

Identify

SC

• Who is my ideal reader?
• What is my purpose for writing?
• What effect do I want to have on my reader?
• What is my subject/theme/topic?

How many ideas can I think of?

Generate

Which is the best idea?

Decide

• What might I say?
• How might I achieve my desired effect?
• What might the reader want/need to know?

BRAIN-STORMING

• What might I include?
• What will have the desired effect?
• What does the reader need to know?
• What conventions of the text are essential to achieve my desired effect?
• How much must I modify those conventions to achieve my desired effect and to make them appropriate for my ideal reader?

• PLANNING
• STRUCTURING
• FIRST DRAFT

Stages that can run simultaneously

Key questions to foster and develop skills specific to the activity

Key visual literacy skills	Key verbal literacy skills
Cropping ● How can we manipulate the image to have the desired effect? ● Does the whole image need to be used? Would a detail of the image be more effective? **Anchoring the meaning** ● How can we use text in conjunction with the image to ensure that the image is read by our ideal reader in the way we intend? **Layout** ● Where can we place the image on the screen or page to catch attention and to create an appropriate relationship with the reader? ● Where do we need to place the text? **Typography** ● How can the presentation of the text contribute to our purpose(s)? ● Could we use colour, vary the size and font to catch attention? ● Can we find a font that captures the urgency of the appeal?	**Word level** ● Can we find words appropriate to our purpose? ● Are there words with emotive connotations that could be used? ● What vocabulary is appropriate to our target audience? **Sentence level** ● What grammatical forms are appropriate to the tone and purpose of this text? ● Are there rhetorical devices that could be used to persuade, such as rhetorical questions, antithesis, exhortation, etc.? ● Are there literary techniques such as alliteration, rhyme, rhythm and figurative language that may be appropriate to our purpose? ● How do we need to adapt the sentence structure to make it appropriate for our audience? **Text level** ● What are the organisational conventions of this text type? (How do we begin? What do we find in the middle of such texts? How do we end?) ● What sort of content is appropriate to this text type?

Introducing the project

In role as Project Director of the World Emergency Relief Organisation (WERO), an imaginary charity, I introduced the pupils to the devastation suffered by Mozambique in February 2000, using data and images taken from Internet sites. Placing the students in the role of campaign strategists, I asked groups of four to devise their own campaign strategy and the materials to be used as part of that strategy, to raise relief money to assist the people of Mozambique. At the end of the activity they would be required to present their campaign to the Director of WERO and the other strategies, explaining and justifying the decisions they had taken.

The project

You are an advertising firm that regularly works for charities. The World Emergency Relief Organisation (WERO) has approached you to devise a national advertising campaign to generate relief funds for Mozambique.

The situation is urgent, so you are under extreme pressure to produce an effective campaign quickly.

The budget proposed for this campaign is £50,000.

Remember that you must accommodate all the costs of the campaign within this budget and make sure that you make a profit. After all, you do this for a living!

There are two elements to this task. You must devise:
● a campaign strategy;
● the materials for the campaign.

You will be required to present and justify your campaign to the publicity officers of WERO.

Gather/organise

What do I know about this?

TASC

The pupils generated a range of questions that they considered as starting points. These were extended with prompts from the teachers so that a framework for thinking emerged.

What do we know about possible target audiences? For example, what newspapers do they read? What television programmes do they watch? Where can they be found or how can they be contacted?

At whom are such campaigns targeted? Children? Teenagers? Working adults? Mothers? Fathers? The retired?

What are the characteristic features of the different types of text used in such campaigns?

What are the disadvantages of using these different types of text?

What sorts of texts are used in such campaigns?

What are the costs and benefits of using these different types of campaign text?

To support their discussion, groups were given materials used by animal charities as exemplars. Many groups chose to produce mind-maps reflecting what they knew. At this point the children were articulating their prior knowledge – intertextual knowledge (i.e. knowledge of the conventions of texts with similar purposes and audiences) and world knowledge – so that it could be mobilised later during the writing process.

Points emerging during the course of discussion included:

● *intertextual knowledge*

   – use pictures
   – pictures often feature a person
   – pictures catch the eye
   – texts have to be memorable
   – the language used appeals to the emotions
   – language 'tricks' – rhyme, rhythm, puns and alliteration are used
   – some information – the most moving facts and details of how money will be used and where to send it – is included
   – television adverts tell stories and use music to make images more moving

● *knowledge of the audience*

   – could reach the target audience at different times through television adverts (e.g. children between 4pm and 6pm)
   – newspapers have different types of reader (the reader of the *Sun* is different from the reader of *The Times*)
   – billboards or handbills posted on cars in car parks are likely to reach people with disposable income (i.e. they have cars)

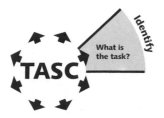

During this stage of the process groups considered in detail the nature of the project. They clarified what they had understood from the briefing about the nature of the ideal reader and their purpose for writing.

The role play and materials taken from the Internet had clearly provided a powerful context for writing. They gave motivation and helpfully established both the notions of writing purpose and of readership or audience. The choice of form was deliberately left open to the groups to decide. This was partly a product of the problem-solving dimension of the task, but it was also out of our desire to cater for different preferred learning styles and the range of intelligences that these children might bring to the task. We wanted to mobilise the strengths that each child had and to engender confidence in writing as a result.

[Catherine] We want as many people as possible to give money.

[Lucy] People who go to work are more likely to have money to spare . . .

[Sarah] It's got to make people notice it . . . and they've got to remember it . . .

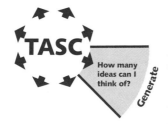

At this point the groups brainstormed possible ideas and approaches. The Gathering and Identification stages had set parameters for this stage. Consequently, without exception, the brainstorming process for each group was focused and purposeful. There was no requirement to record the outcomes of brainstorming in a specific way. Again, many groups produced mindmaps. However, one interesting variation involved the group arranging on its desk a range of possible pictures to be used, over which scraps of paper were placed identifying individual words or phrases that might accompany them.

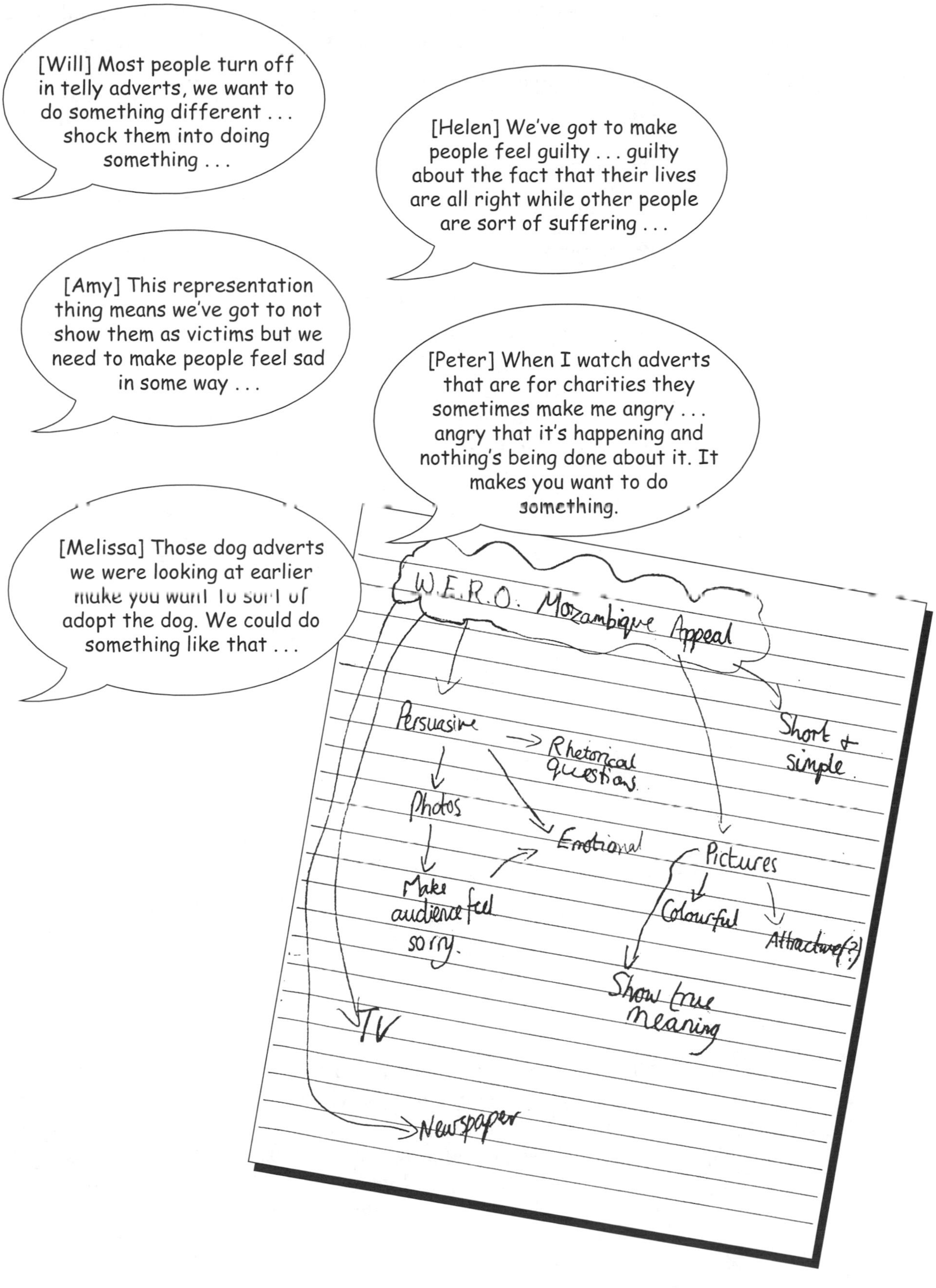

[Will] Most people turn off in telly adverts, we want to do something different . . . shock them into doing something . . .

[Helen] We've got to make people feel guilty . . . guilty about the fact that their lives are all right while other people are sort of suffering . . .

[Amy] This representation thing means we've got to not show them as victims but we need to make people feel sad in some way . . .

[Peter] When I watch adverts that are for charities they sometimes make me angry . . . angry that it's happening and nothing's being done about it. It makes you want to do something.

[Melissa] Those dog adverts we were looking at earlier make you want to sort of adopt the dog. We could do something like that . . .

W.E.R.O. Mozambique Appeal

Persuasive → Rhetorical questions

Short & simple.

Photos

Emotional

Pictures

Make audience feel sorry.

Colourful

Attractive(?)

Show true meaning

TV

Newspaper

Groups considered a wide range of possibilities. All of the following emerged during the initial discussions:

● newspaper adverts

● targeted mail shots

● billboard posters

● handbills

● national radio appeals

● national television appeals

Interestingly, at this stage most groups revealed a considerable sharpening of thought. For example, the generalised notion of persuasion that had featured during the Gathering stage had turned into a discussion of particular ways of persuading: specific emotions were identified as appropriate writing goals.

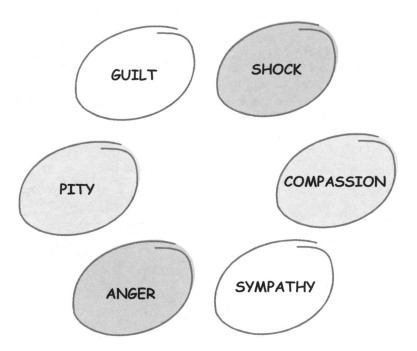

Although the Generation stage meant that most groups had more than one possible approach to the project, groups needed a specific proposal on which to proceed. In other activities during the week, the decision stage had proven problematic. Many of the children on the summer school were highly able and passionate guardians of their own ideas. Decisions regarding the best idea had been difficult to arrive at. On this occasion, however, the criteria by which the decision could be made had emerged during the identification stage:

● Will it be persuasive?

● Will it stick in the minds of the target audience?

- Will it catch the attention of the target audience?

- What does the target audience need to know?

- Is it manageable with the provided resources?

- Is it manageable within the deadline?

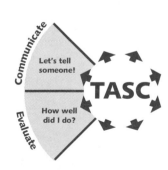

[Carol] If we want mums and dads to give money we have to have the pictures with the children in them.

[Anne] We need to show that people are hungry and that millions have been affected ... so we will have to say something like ...

[Kylie] If we are aiming this at children they watch things like *EastEnders* and *Emmerdale* so you could put it on telly a bit later ...

[Dean] We've only got £50,000 so we can't do television and newspapers, we have to choose the one that is going to be seen by most people.

[Colin] I don't think it sounds right in an advert for a charity giving away a prize ... that's all right for things that you are **selling** but it doesn't seem right for giving money.

The evaluation stage in writing is not a single, self-contained stage. In this activity it permeated both the implementation stage and the communication stage. During the collaborative writing of the campaign materials, the children constantly asked each other questions such as:

Does that sound all right?

Are there too many words on this page?

Do you think this looks okay?

Can you read this and see if it's the right sort of thing?

Do you think that's the right picture to begin with?

Thus, ideas were constantly challenged using the criteria that had evolved during the Decision phase.

[Helen] We want to make people feel sad. Talking about lots of people won't work. We want to tell a story like in the fruit pastille advert . . . We want a name and tell someone's story of what happened in the floods . . .

[Celia] Hang on, if you're driving past a poster you don't want that many words, do you?

[Graham] No . . . no . . . no . . . you want something that sticks in the mind . . . you want something like 'Don't delay. Give today.' That sticks in the mind. It rhymes.

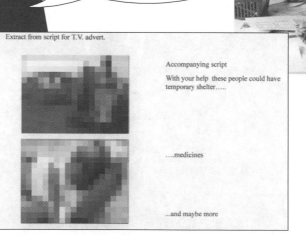

Extract from script for T.V. advert.

Accompanying script

With your help these people could have temporary shelter.....

....medicines

...and maybe more

Furthermore, part of the overall activity required each group to justify its campaign strategy to the project director and competing campaign strategists. This requirement clearly contributed to the quality of the outcomes and of the learning; it placed pressure on groups to apply consciously their knowledge and understanding of the generic features of their chosen form and to make explicit the links between the features of their text and their notions of audience and purpose. It also provided a purposeful context for immediate feedback on the effectiveness of the materials: groups entered into a dialogue with readers regarding what worked and what did not.

[Susan] I think that's really good, because you don't expect it . . . It makes you think.

[Richard] I think you need to have put the bit about where to send the money at the end . . . it's the last thing people should see . . . if you put it earlier then you haven't persuaded people. You have to persuade people first and then tell them what to do. Most adverts that I've seen on the telly, the last thing you see is like a telephone number or an address or something . . .

[Rachel] In a TV advert it's the pictures you remember . . . I think you have used too many words. The only words you really want are the address and the telephone number.

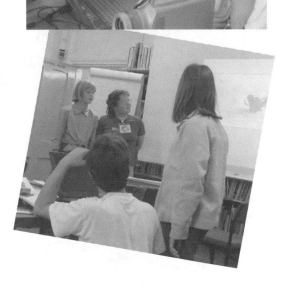

The outcomes

The outcomes were extremely impressive. High quality finished products were accompanied by thoughtful justification. One particularly effective presentation was played to the accompaniment *of The Earth is Never Satisfied* by Ladysmith Black Mambazo to the absolute silence of all in the room: a true testimony to its effectiveness.

Mozambique Mayhem

Today over 150,000 are at risk because of the heavy downpours. With your help we could reduce that number considerably. Even a small donation can help us buy the necessities so that the residence of Mozambique can get back to a normal life.

Donate now - every little helps

Just think before you buy an expensive outfit you do not really need! The money you spend could help a family like the Ashwiwua family survive the torrential rain and diseases. Help them now before they die like thousands of other unfortunate people.

Budget

- Spending:-
- Computing=£6000
- Adverts in
  paper=£27900
- Pictures=£2200

Appeal Planning

- Budget expenditure.
- Adverts.

Our Slogan

- Give us a fiver, Help the Mozambique survivors.

Mozambique

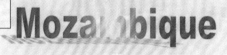

- Actual advert.
- Appeal planning.
- Budget.
- Pictures (some may be disturbing).

W.E.R.O

This is a small child, a survivor of the disastrous and terrible floods in Mozambique.

As you can see, the conditions are terrible and those who survive face disease.

All they need are the basic tools and equipment to survive. We need £15m to provide this for them. Please give us all the money you can spear. Send your donations to:-

W.E.R.O
Mozambique flood appeal
FREEPOST
PO Box 712
London E1 8ZZ   Tel. 01 21 897 987 675

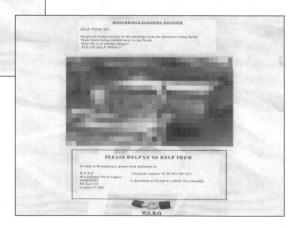

MOZAMBIQUE FLOODING DISASTER

HELP THEM BY

People are dying everyday in Mozambique from the disastrous rising floods.
Their food is being washed away in the floods.
Their life is in extreme danger!
PLEASE HELP THEM!!!

PLEASE HELP US TO HELP THEM

To help in Mozambique, please send donations to:

W.E.R.O   Telephone number: 01 02 897 987 673
Mozambique Flood Appeal
FREEPOST   A minimum of £2 and we will be very thankful.
PO Box 712
London E1 8ZZ

W.E.R.O

Pictures

Mathematical Makeovers:
Using Existing Mathematics Problems to Promote the Development of Thinking Skills

JEANETTE BROCKS, MELISA BAYLISS and SUE FOSTER-AGG

Mathematics equips pupils with a uniquely powerful set of tools to understand and change the world. These tools include logical reasoning, problem-solving skills, and the ability to think in abstract ways . . .

Mathematics is a creative discipline. It can stimulate moments of pleasure and wonder when a pupil solves a problem for the first time, discovers a more elegant solution to that problem, or suddenly sees hidden connections. (DfEE/QCA 1999)

PURPOSE

We are in the midst of a major national initiative to raise pupils' achievement in mathematics through improving the quality of teaching and learning at Key Stages 1, 2 and 3. The National Numeracy Strategy (NNS) describes numeracy as a proficiency children acquire through being taught mathematics well. It is not just about basic arithmetic.

> The outcome should be numerate pupils who are confident enough to tackle mathematical problems without going immediately to teachers or friends for help. (DfEE 1999c)
>
> Numeracy . . . requires understanding of the number system, a repertoire of mathematical techniques, and an inclination and ability to solve quantitative or spatial problems in a range of contexts. (DfEE 2001)

There is a clear relationship between thinking skills and using and applying mathematics. Using and Applying Mathematics (UAM) is part of the statutory requirement of the National Curriculum for mathematics and so constitutes an important strand in the NNS.

> Thinking skills underpin using and applying mathematics and the broad strands of problem solving, communication and reasoning. Well chosen mathematical activities will develop pupils' thinking skills.
>
> (DfEE 2001)

This chapter considers how the TASC approach can provide a teaching and learning strategy that will promote pupils' mathematical thinking and so improve their ability to solve problems.

 **COMMENT** ▶

Developing pupils' ability to use and apply their mathematics and their thinking skills should be an integral part of everyday teaching, not a 'bolt-on' activity. In order to promote links within mathematics and provide contexts for UAM, National Curriculum 2000 embeds the three strands of the programme of study for UAM (problem-solving, communicating and reasoning) in the other programmes of study.

Pupils need a variety of experiences, and mathematics lessons that focus on 'an investigation', especially if linked directly with a current mathematics topic or 'real-life' context, can play a purposeful role in focusing pupils' and teachers' attention on 'using and applying' or thinking skills and provide valuable and exciting opportunities for children to:

- work cooperatively and talk about mathematics;

- make connections between different ideas within mathematics;

- develop their mathematical reasoning and thinking skills;

- apply their mathematics to a range of contexts, including the wider curriculum and everyday life, as well as exploration within mathematics itself; and so

- enhance their learning in mathematics.

Investigative activities present an ideal context for introducing TASC to the mathematics classroom.

Following the Cockcroft report (Cockcroft 1982), which like the NNS also promoted a variety of learning opportunities for children, a large number of publications with ideas for 'investigations' were written. These books, often produced by LEAs, may have lacked the glossy finish of more recent publications, but they contained a wealth of ideas for investigative activities. Some consisted of ideas and starting points for mathematics investigations, others also included *guidance* for teachers in how to introduce and develop the activities. These activities are still around: in some cases, part of the teacher's valuable repertoire; or reworked and supplemented in new publications; or perhaps gathering dust in the mathematics coordinator's cupboard. *They provide the ideal material for a 'mathematical makeover' using a thinking skills approach.*

This chapter includes teachers' accounts of three lessons, based on old favourites, which were perfect for the makeover treatment. The purpose of this section is to look at how a familiar mathematical problem-solving task can be used alongside the TASC model to structure a successful mathematics lesson. Links to the Frameworks for teaching mathematics (Reception to Year 6; Years 7, 8, and 9) are clear, demonstrating that thinking skills lessons like these can be integral, and need not be an 'add-on' to daily mathematics teaching.

As questioning plays such a key role in determining the quality of teaching and learning, our work on interpreting the TASC Wheel as a structure for supporting problem-solving and investigative work in mathematics centred on devising questions for each stage.

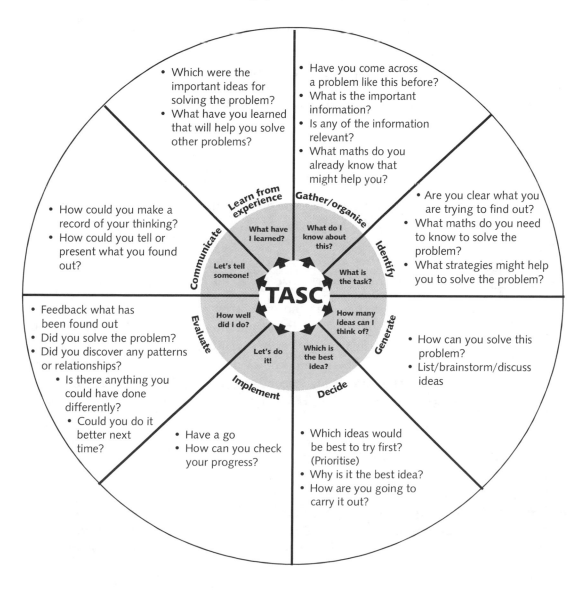

The following section illustrates how the TASC Wheel was used to plan and teach three lessons, entirely consistent with the NNS, for pupils in Years 5–7.

Investigation 1: Max Box

PURPOSE

Activity

Easter was approaching, so I gave this familiar 'Max Box'-type puzzle a seasonal focus. The children were challenged to make a box from one sheet of A4 card that would hold as many mini-eggs as possible. The children were told that, at a later date, they would make a lid for the box, so the surface of the eggs could not be higher than the sides of the box.

Objectives

(Taken directly from the National Numeracy Framework, 2000 (DfEE 1999c))

● Solve mathematical problems, recognise and explain patterns and relationships, generalise and predict.

● Explain methods and reasoning.

● Explain a generalised relationship (formula) in words.

● Suggest suitable units and measuring equipment to estimate and measure capacity.

● Understand area measured in square centimetres

● Understand and use the formula in words 'length × breadth' for the area of a rectangle.

COMMENT

The Oral and Mental Starter: Area Bingo

Each mathematics pair chose six area measurements from a selection on the board to put into their bingo grid on their mini white board. I then turned over cards revealing a length and width measurement. Using their prior knowledge of 'length × width = area', the children then had a few seconds to calculate the area and cross off appropriate answers to reach a 'full house'.

Using the TASC Wheel

Having posed the problem, I asked the children to predict the maximum number of mini-eggs a box could hold. Individuals were keen to offer estimates; this question immediately got them involved and thinking about the challenge ahead. Their suggestions ranged from 25 to 98 as they tried to visualise the end product filled with mini-eggs.

As a class, the children suggested links with problems they had come across before. They remembered a Christmas design and technology project that had involved making a container for biscuits using a net.

As the children discussed the problem, I asked them what the important information in the problem was. Was there any irrelevant information? Emma suggested that it did not matter that it was mini-eggs; the biggest box would be the biggest box regardless. This line of thinking led the class to conclude that it was actually *capacity* that they needed to find out.

As the children contributed to a class list of information they already knew that might help them in this challenge, the idea of calculating the area of a base of a box by using length multiplied by width was suggested.

The children were given three minutes to work with their partners to discuss the mathematics they could use to solve this problem along with the strategies they might employ. A variety of different approaches emerged:

● Some children sketched in order to illustrate their idea for their partner.

● Other children reached for props around them to demonstrate their point.

● Simon talked to his partner James about the possibility of using a formula to work out what the maximum capacity *could* be before actually designing a box.

● The idea of making a box by cutting out the corners of a rectangle was suggested.

The children offered their ideas, and a class list of useful suggestions was compiled.

Discussion had taken place; sharing and some refinement of ideas had been the result. Although concluding which was the best idea from the suggested list may work at this stage in the Wheel in some situations, I decided against it. Through discussion the children had formed and developed their own ideas and strategies. It was clear that the class list actually represented different mathematics pairs accessing the activity at different levels, starting their problem-solving from a point that was relevant to their previous learning and appropriate to their ability.

The children were keen to have a go. They were given a time limit of 30 minutes to work with their mathematics partner to create their box. This section of the lesson provided me with a wonderful opportunity to watch and listen to different groups.

As the pairs busily discussed their ideas, language was key as the children communicated and developed their ideas. I was able to move around the groups stimulating the children's thinking through my questioning.

This section of the lesson also provided valuable and interesting opportunities for informal assessment through both observation and questioning.

As the children worked in their groups and I took on the role of observer, I was able to listen to discussion between mathematics partners. Many of the children were beginning to demonstrate self-questioning techniques. This was apparent at different levels, but even the basic 'Well, why . . . ?' prompted explanations, use of vocabulary, refining of ideas and a realisation of potential problems with the process or design.

The idea of a senior learner inducting an apprentice junior learner into different styles of thinking also took place within the groups. In the case of Simon and James, both able mathematicians, Simon was able to model and demonstrate the ideas and thinking surrounding his formulaic approach to calculating the largest possible capacity.

The involvement of *all* the children in this mixed ability class at different levels was also evident. Although the children who were working on this problem present a range of different strengths and weaknesses, every child was focused, tackling the task enthusiastically. The variety of approaches and the different levels in sophistication in thinking were remarkable.

The children were brought together briefly and asked one further question:

How do you *know* if you have made the box that would hold the most mini-eggs?

This prompted lots of discussion *between* groups, as different groups developed strategies for testing and comparing the capacity of their boxes. Again, the sophistication of these strategies varied significantly.

- For many of the class, multilink was the obvious substitute for mini-eggs; they could compare the capacity of their boxes without the need for mini-eggs.

- One pair tested the capacity of their box by filling it with multilink, counting as they placed the cubes inside.

- Another pair put a column of four multilink inside their box and could then see, with the visual prompt in front of them, that they needed four of these columns in total.

- A common strategy among many of the children was to *begin* filling their boxes, perhaps with one row or one 'layer', but they then realised that they could use calculations to work out the capacity rather than filling the whole box!

- Simon and James had been basing their design on Simon's previous knowledge of 'length × width × height' and had therefore calculated the capacity of the box they made in centimetres cubed, using the formula.

$$6 \times 9 \times 17 = 918 \text{ cm}^3$$
$$7 \times 7 \times 15 = 737 \text{ cm}^3$$
$$8 \times 5 \times 13 = 520 \text{ cm}^3$$
$$9 \times 8 \times 11 = 297 \text{ cm}^3$$
$$4 \times 13 \times 21 = 1092 \text{ cm}^3$$
$$3 \times 15 \times 23 = 1035 \text{ cm}^3$$
$$2 \times 17 \times 25 = 850 \text{ cm}^3$$
$$1 \times 19 \times 27 = 513 \text{ cm}^3$$

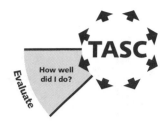

The children came together to discuss and evaluate the range of strategies and thinking that had emerged.

The ethos of the class was particularly important in this respect. Essentially, the children were secure in knowing that it was fine to offer and be proud of strategies and ideas (although they clearly reflected varying abilities or different preferred approaches to learning).

When I asked the class how well they had done, the children clearly felt that, although they might not have created the box with *the* largest capacity, they *were* successful. By working through the stages of the TASC Wheel they had achieved.

The groups were keen to share their strategies and discoveries with the rest of the class and as they did this, three main approaches to tackling the problem emerged.

Several groups of children had made a box straight away, with little discussion *beforehand* about what might make a large capacity. As they worked, they discussed and discovered how they could improve their design.

Other groups discussed, modelled or sketched ideas before creating a net.

Simon and James worked logically through different combinations of possible widths, lengths and heights to create the largest capacity.

The bigger the base the larger the capacity even if the sides do get smaller.

There might be a limit to how big the base can be before the capacity starts going down again.

As the class presented their strategies, it was the children presenting who acted as the senior learners, modelling their thinking processes. As they discussed what they had learned, common relationships and patterns emerged, again reflecting different levels of, and approaches to, thinking:

- Some of the children discovered that if they cut corners off an A4 sheet to make a net, the corners they cut had to be square in shape, as cutting rectangles meant the box would have sides of different heights.

- All of the children realised that in order to calculate capacity using multilink, they did not actually have to *fill* the box with multilink; they could use 'length × width = area' to calculate how many would be in each layer.

- As the next step, many children were then able to make the connection with the formula 'length × width × height = capacity' as I modelled this working using their boxes and their measurements.

Almost *every* pair had ideas for something they could have done differently and would do better next time. Again, their comments reflected different abilities:

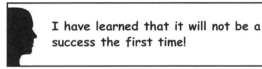

> I have learned that it will not be a success the first time!

Natasha, a less confident mathematician, reflected on her trial and improvement approach. This realisation reflected the opportunities provided by the structure of the TASC Wheel to question and modify.

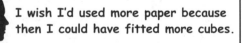

> I wish I'd used more paper because then I could have fitted more cubes.

Susan started with a small net in the centre of her A4 squared paper. This simple realisation demonstrated significant progress and learning for Susan.

The class compiled a list of things that *they* felt they had learned during the lesson, with me acting as scribe.

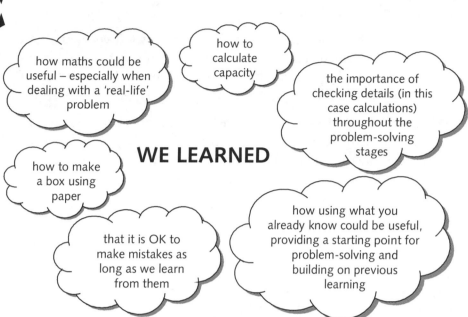

WE LEARNED

- how maths could be useful – especially when dealing with a 'real-life' problem
- how to calculate capacity
- the importance of checking details (in this case calculations) throughout the problem-solving stages
- how to make a box using paper
- that it is OK to make mistakes as long as we learn from them
- how using what you already know could be useful, providing a starting point for problem-solving and building on previous learning

My reflections

As a teacher new to the TASC Wheel, I was surprised by the extent to which it acted as an enabler to me and the children in many different ways.

- It provided the structure for a problem that I would have previously used with my class. It was this structure that allowed me to feel confident that I was successfully maximising the children's learning on this mathematical concept, and also in terms of thinking skills that would, with practice, be transferable and applicable in other areas of maths and the wider curriculum.

- The progression through the stages of the TASC Wheel made this 'real-life' challenge accessible to all abilities. *All* the children were enabled by the development and progression in thinking that the wheel takes every individual through.

- There had been no need for differentiation in the initial challenge given to the class. With the key questions that I discussed with the class in the stages of the TASC Wheel, all children were given the opportunity to develop their thinking from their own starting point.

- If learning is to be maximised and beneficial to all of the children, I will need to continue to foster an ethos within my classroom where all children are valued as problem-solvers and thinkers, and feel confident to 'take risks' with their thinking.

- The progression of the wheel allowed me to make explicit to the children the problem-solving process and the thinking skills that are integral to it. I was able to model my own thinking processes out loud to the children throughout the lesson, often through my questioning.

- This links to the idea of having a senior learner demonstrating different thinking styles to the apprentice junior learner who, with practice, will be able to adopt the strategies themselves. Through this, I was helping the children to reinforce what they know *and* how they are learning. My aim is that the children, with further practice and guidance, will begin to transfer skills and strategies to new situations and contexts both within mathematics and in other curriculum areas.

Investigation 2: Swaps

 PURPOSE

This problem was set to a group of mixed ability Year 6 children as the TASC Wheel was introduced. Its starting point was the NNS objective:

> Solve mathematical problems or puzzles, recognise and explain patterns and relationships, generalise and predict. Suggest extensions be asking 'What if . . .?'

 **COMMENT**

The oral mental starter to this lesson was a visualisation exercise to start children thinking. The children were shown the grid overleaf and asked questions such as:

Where will the square be if the two end columns swap? If the diagonal corners swap places?

What will be in the top right-hand corner if the grid changes along the centre diagonal from top left to top right? What will be in the centre? What will be in the middle square of the left-hand column?

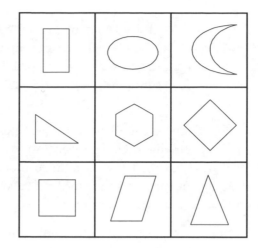

The children were presented with their first view of the mathematical thinking Wheel and given the following task:

Three boys and three girls are seated alternately in a row. By swapping adjacent children, change the seating arrangement so that the boys are sitting together and the girls are sitting together in as few moves as possible. How many moves does it take?

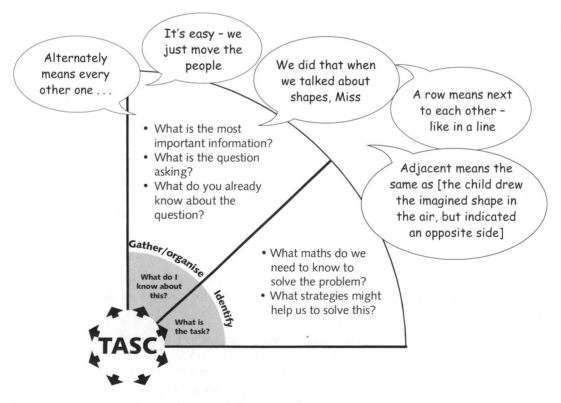

At this point, several of the more able pupils were convinced that they knew how to carry this out. They had identified no strategies, but had gone for one solid idea. Other pupils were more open and inclined to pose possible solutions.

TASC

How many ideas can I think of?

Generate

- How can we solve this problem?
- How would we sit them?

We could draw the pattern out and move the pieces

Why don't we sit down and try it?

With the boys at one end and the girls at the other?

No, we said adjacent meant right next to so each boy will have to sit next to a girl

TASC

Which is the best idea?

Decide

Children of different abilities took turns in trying to physically direct six children, then eight, then ten, to see how many moves it took to change the seating arrangements. This proved to be great fun and caused lots of laughter and mutual support as children experimented to find the least number of moves.

TASC

Let's do it!

Implement

Right, Mark change places with Jane; Jane change places with Katy. Mmmm ...No ...Go back ...Start again. Jane, stay where you are. Mark change places with Katy; Brian, change places with Lizzie. Now Mark change places with Lizzie. That's Jane, Katy, Lizzie, Mark, Brian and Oliver. That's three moves.

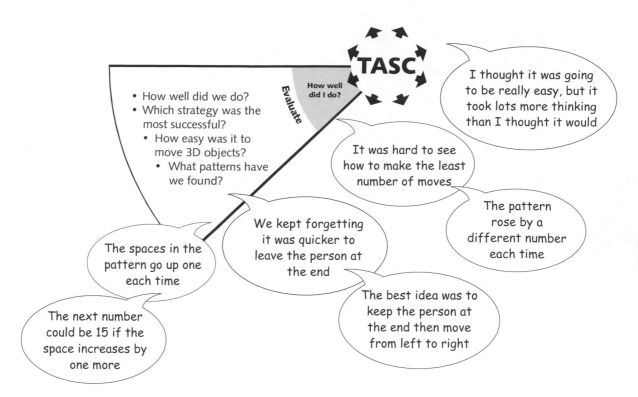

- How well did we do?
- Which strategy was the most successful?
- How easy was it to move 3D objects?
- What patterns have we found?

I thought it was going to be really easy, but it took lots more thinking than I thought it would

It was hard to see how to make the least number of moves

The pattern rose by a different number each time

We kept forgetting it was quicker to leave the person at the end

The spaces in the pattern go up one each time

The best idea was to keep the person at the end then move from left to right

The next number could be 15 if the space increases by one more

Pattern found		
Number of children		Number of moves
6	→	3
8	→	6
10	→	10

An important part of mathematics is extending thinking with 'What if . . .?' questions:

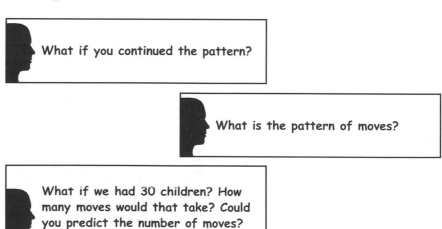

What if you continued the pattern?

What is the pattern of moves?

What if we had 30 children? How many moves would that take? Could you predict the number of moves?

COMMENT ▶

These questions were explored using two different coloured counters. The room buzzed with excitement.

- Can you record your learning for someone else to try?

Communicate

Let's tell someone!

TASC

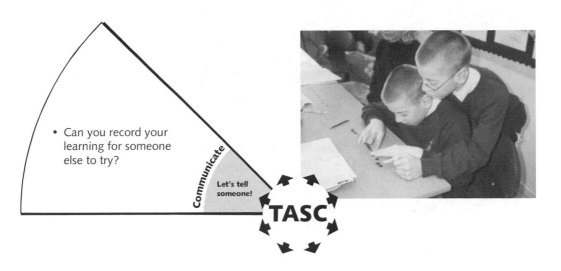

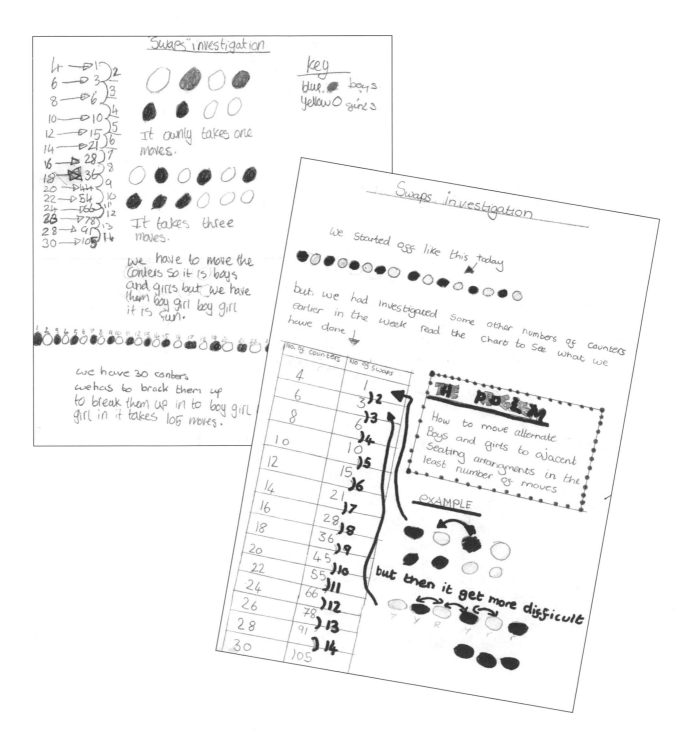

My reflections

● In this situation the less able were exemplars for the more able on recording. The more able went straight to the pattern, which did not explain the process.

● The level of logical thinking was higher than the group had previously demonstrated because they followed the structure of the TASC Wheel.

● The self-esteem of the less able rose because they had that support.

● Several more able boys found recording a real problem and consequently made inaccuracies in their calculations. They became frustrated. These were boys who tried to jump straight from the task set to the solution without actually thinking through the process.

● The physical and numerical link supported the learning processes enabling all children to identify the pattern, discuss it and quantify it.

● The spatial problem of moving 3D objects and reasoning was challenging. The more able coped far better than the less able and boys were generally better than girls.

 **COMMENT** ▶ One child is worthy of a specific mention. She developed her own explanation of a pattern. She began by identifying how many moves four counters would take and looked at the patterns made, seeing the following:

Number of counters		Number of moves	Pattern
4	→	1	$\frac{1}{4}$
6	→	3	$\frac{3}{6} = \frac{1}{2} = \frac{2}{4}$
8	→	6	$\frac{6}{8} = \frac{3}{4}$
10	→	10	$\frac{10}{10} = \frac{4}{4}$
12	→	15	$\frac{15}{12} = \frac{5}{4}$

This demonstrated an understanding of fractions, their relationship to each other and an awareness of pattern. She was also able to teach the pattern she had found to the class and three adults within it. She explained her thinking processes clearly to the audience, enabling the class to understand and appreciate her success with unprompted clapping.

This child is more able but has little faith in her mathematical ability and finds making links between learning difficult in this subject. The TASC process guided and supported her but gave her the permission to experiment in this extension of the problem.

> **What if the counters were in a square? What if there were two rows of counters?**

> I tried this. I had 16 coloured dots in four colours arranged in a square. If I move these dots from the bottom to the top it takes 12 moves.

Investigation 3: Painted Cube

● **PURPOSE**   This investigation was introduced to pupils in the top set in both Year 6 and Year 7. The characteristics displayed by more able youngsters in mathematics would suggest that these youngsters have particular strengths in problem-solving. Does the structure of the TASC Wheel still have something to offer?

Objectives (key objectives in bold type) Year 6	Year 7
Solve mathematical problems, recognise and explain patterns and relationships, generalise and predict. Suggest extensions asking 'What if . . .?' **Explain methods and reasoning.** Develop from explaining a generalised relationship in words to expressing it in a formula using letters as symbols. Describe and visualise properties of solid shapes . . .	**Solve word problems and investigate in a range of contexts (number, algebra, shape and space . . .)** Identify the necessary information to solve a problem; represent problems mathematically, using words, diagrams, tables . . . Present and interpret solutions in the context of the original problem; **explain and justify methods and conclusions,** orally and in writing. Suggest extensions by asking 'What if . . .?' or 'Why . . .?'; begin to generalise.

The painted cube

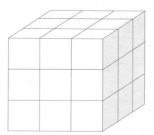

Imagine this cube (a 4 × 4 × 4 cube was used with Year 7 pupils) sprayed with gold paint, then dropped on the floor so it falls apart. What would the multilink cubes look like? How many cubes would have one, two, three . . . of their faces sprayed? Investigate for different cubes.

Oral and mental starter

I chose activities to encourage visualisation and revise the vocabulary of 3D shape. For Year 6, this involved children taking turns to imagine a 3D shape (I modelled this initially) and the rest of the class asking questions until they could guess the shape (only questions requiring Yes or No answers were allowed!).

3D shapes were available and flashcards were on display to prompt children to use precise vocabulary.

For the Year 7 lesson, I used an overhead projector to project a net of a cube with different coloured faces on to a screen. The children were encouraged to visualise the net folded to make a cube and then asked questions.

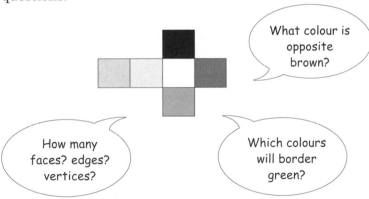

Next, an overhead transparency of a selection of hexominoes was displayed.

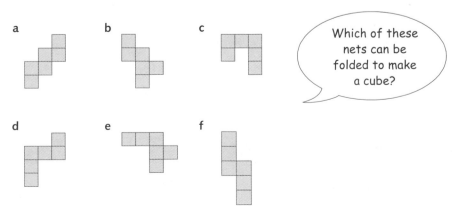

The children were encouraged to work with a partner and justify their choices.

A model of the Wheel was used, building up the stages piece by piece, and introduced to the children as a strategy to help them solve problems.

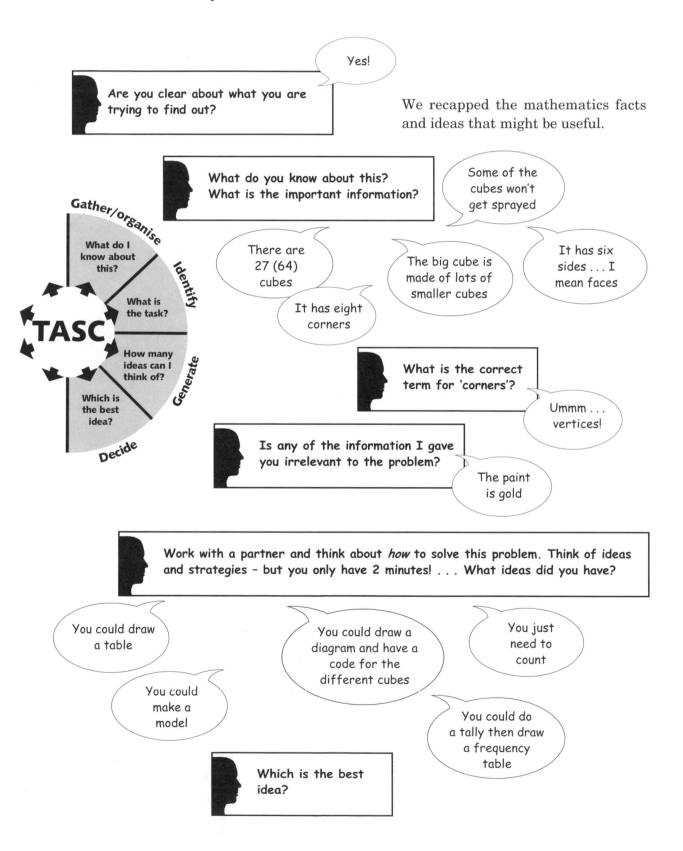

We recapped the mathematics facts and ideas that might be useful.

What is the task?

To find out how many faces of so many cubes have been painted gold. – this is a 4 x 4 x 4 cube.
Then look at different cubes.

What do I already know?

The vertices will have 3 faces painted, the cubes on the edges will have 2 faces painted, the cubes in the middle will have 1 face painted. There are 64 cubes.

The investigation

The 8 in the middle will have no faces painted.
The 8 vertices will have 3 faces painted.
The 24 on the edges not including the vertices will have 2 sides painted.
The 4 cubes on each side in the middle of each face have 1 side painted which equals 24.
Then I add them all together 24 + 24 + 8 + 8 = 64 cubes
so . . . .
24 cubes have 1 side painted
24 cubes have 2 sides painted
8 cubes have 3 sides painted
8 cubes have 0 sides painted

My reflections

● The first stage was a useful opportunity to revise the properties of a cube and rehearse the precise use of vocabulary (faces, edges, vertices). These Year 7 girls chose to note down this information and reported finding it useful.

● Asking the pupils to discuss possible strategies in pairs, and then share the ideas, was valuable.

● It was interesting that the children itching to get going had actually interpreted the problem differently and much more superficially, having not engaged in the *Identify* stage.

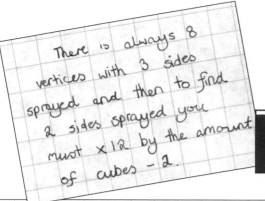

There is always 8 vertices with 3 sides sprayed and then to find 2 sides sprayed you must ×12 by the amount of cubes – 2.

What have you learned that will help you to solve other problems? Which were the important ideas?

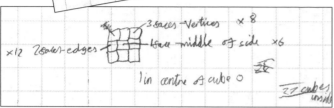

What if you start with a different cube?

Tallying took a long time. We'll just do the table next time

Could you do it better next time? Is there anything you could have done differently?

How well did you do? Did you solve the problem?

The corner cubes have three gold faces and the edge cubes always have two

Did you discover any patterns or relationships?

Let's do it! Choose your strategy and have a go!

TASC

Learn from experience

What have I learned?

Let's tell someone!

Communicate

How well did I do?

Evaluate

Let's do it!

Implement

Emma and Lucy devised an ingenious colour coding system to indicate the number of faces that would be sprayed. They then rebuilt the 3 × 3 × 3 cube using their system.

My reflections

● Children generally chose to follow through their own ideas at the *Implementation* stage, working in groups of two or three, and it was a useful opportunity to circulate, probe pupils' thinking and encourage sharing of ideas between groups when this seemed to be productive. The children in both classes worked with enthusiasm!

● A wide range of recording was produced, both in terms of presentation format chosen and clarity of expression.

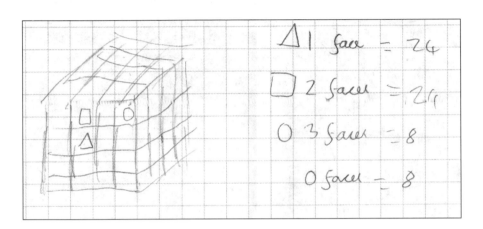

△ 1 face = 24

□ 2 faces = 24

○ 3 faces = 8

0 faces = 8

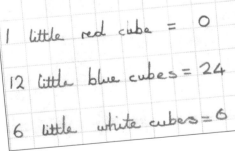

Red = none

Yellow = 3

Blue = 2

White = 1

8 little Yellow cubes = 24

1 little red cube = 0

12 little blue cubes = 24

6 little white cubes = 6

edges	16	24 edges with 2 sides painted each
vertices	8	8 with 3 sides painted
faces	24	24 with 1 side painted.
		8 with 0 painted.

Results.

		Evaluation.
2 painted	24 cubes	I thought the idea worked
3 painted	8 cubes	well and I shall use it
1 painted	24 cubes	again on the 10×10 cube.
0 painted	8 cubes	

My reflections

● The initial stages, *Gather/organise* and *Identify*, provided a useful opportunity for assessment and showed that while we, as teachers, may make the links between ideas, pupils (even more able pupils) may not, unless we help them to do this. It also helped to establish the *language* that would support the problem-solving. Some of the more able boys appeared to find these stages frustrating, and were eager to get 'stuck in' to the problem, but then had difficulties later when they realised they had insufficient understanding of the problem, so had to go back a step.

● Several pupils later reported finding the *Generate* and *Decide* stages useful for thinking through their ideas and found that they gave them some alternative strategies to go back to if they got stuck, or a strategy for checking their results. Again, these stages provided a useful opportunity for assessment, which also helped to raise pupils' (and the teacher's!) awareness of the range of strategies available. Some children surprised their teachers!

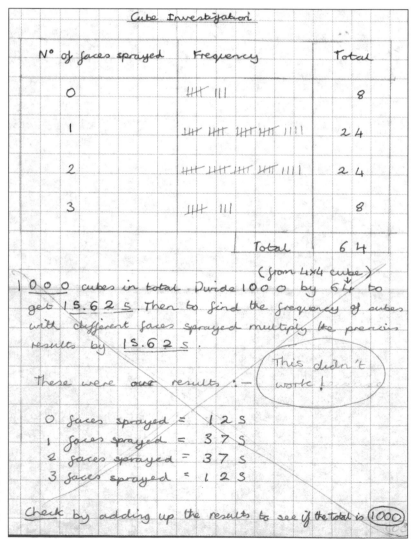

One group of girls used another group's method to check their thinking. This was a useful opportunity to discuss why their strategy was flawed *and* to reassure them that they hadn't wasted their time and effort!

- The teacher plays a key role in observing and questioning during the *Implement* stage. Planning some questions in advance that encourage children to explain and justify their strategies, their thinking, their choice of methods of recording and their results is useful. Such questions can then be used to challenge pupils as well as offer support.

- The *Evaluate* stage, as well as providing an opportunity to look at results, was useful for considering the range of strategies and their efficiency, and for making the link with the properties of a cube. The Year 6 children used a range of strategies, including some powerful visual representations. In the Year 7 lesson, the chance for a pupil to model an explanation of the relationships he had identified *in words*, helped to clarify other pupils' thinking and was a valuable precursor to expressing the relationship algebraically. It was a clearer explanation of the relationship between the faces, edges and vertices of the cube and the number of smaller cubes with different numbers of faces sprayed, than I could have given myself. The algebraic expressions were then so easy!

- The process promoted key experiences for children's understanding in algebra – the ability to visualise, to make links and explore patterns (spatial and numerical) and relationships, to express these relationships and any generalisations made verbally and in the context of the problem.

- The Year 7 pupils took the investigation much further than the Year 6 set and the task clearly matched the NNS objectives identified for each year group. The investigation could be tackled at different levels across the middle years, as an enrichment opportunity for more able Year 6 pupils, or in Key Stage 3.

- A few children chose to work individually and did so effectively. Encouraging these children to share their ideas with each other was important, so that they had an opportunity to verbalise and justify their thinking.

Jenny worked alone, imagining the cube 'sliced' vertically. She devised a diagram to represent each layer of the cube, and she was then able to represent her results in a table (see overleaf). This would have led to some interesting patterns if more time had been available.

Number of Sides covered in paint on each cube.

front			Middle			Back		
→3	2	3	2	1	2	3	2	3
2	1	2	1	0	1	2	1	2
3	2	3	2	1	2	3	2	3

9 cubes   9 cubes   9 cubes

altogether 27 cubes.

	Front,	Middle	Back	altogether.	
1 side	1	4	1	6	26 sides coloured
2 sides	4	4	4	12	
3 sides	4	0	4	8	

sides coloured.

Question · Solve mathematical problems, reconise and explain patterns and relationships, generalise and predict. Suggest extensions. Ask 'What if......?'

Question · Use same stratigy with a two by three cubiod.

Number of sides coverd in paint on each cube

front		Middle		Back	
→3	3	2	2	3	3
3	3	2	2	3	3

altogether 12 cubes

	front	Middle	Back	altogether	
2 sides	0	4	0	4	12 sides coloured
3 sides	4	0	4	8	

sides coloured.

● The final stage, *Learn from experience*, prompted some useful ideas from the children, but effectiveness in promoting *transfer* can't be evaluated from a single lesson.

Conclusion

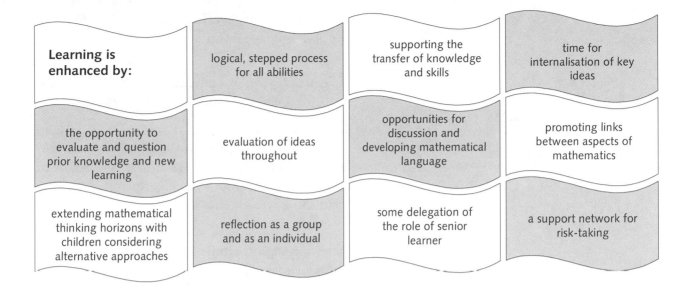

Learning is enhanced by:	logical, stepped process for all abilities	supporting the transfer of knowledge and skills	time for internalisation of key ideas
the opportunity to evaluate and question prior knowledge and new learning	evaluation of ideas throughout	opportunities for discussion and developing mathematical language	promoting links between aspects of mathematics
extending mathematical thinking horizons with children considering alternative approaches	reflection as a group and as an individual	some delegation of the role of senior learner	a support network for risk-taking

Read the lesson reports.

GROUP DISCUSSION

How did the TASC Wheel support the teachers in:

● planning and organising the lesson?

● using a range of lower and higher order questions?

● providing an appropriate challenge for children of different abilities and learning styles?

● taking and delegating the role of 'senior learner'?

How did the TASC Wheel support children:

● in developing their mathematical thinking and problem-solving abilities?

● if they got stuck?

● in taking the role of 'senior learner'?

To what extent do these teachers' experiences relate to your own?

REFLECT

Are there aspects of your classroom practice you could develop using these insights?

National Strategies

The NNS was launched in 1999 for Key Stages 1 and 2, and the mathematics element of the Key Stage 3 NNS was launched in 2001. The following are some of the elements of the NNS's guidance relevant to this chapter:

- *Lively direct interactive teaching* is advocated: 'A two-way process in which pupils are expected to play an active part . . .'

- The *structure* of the mathematics lesson is emphasised, with an *oral and mental starter* to rehearse and apply skills, a *main teaching activity* with clear objectives, flexibility of organisation and variety of activities, and a *plenary* to reflect on the lesson, summarise the key elements and make links to other work.

- The importance of developing pupils' *mathematical language* and correct use of vocabulary is stressed.

- The importance of *making links* within mathematics, and between mathematics and other subjects is emphasised.

- *Using and applying mathematics* (UAM) is integrated throughout. In Key Stages 1 and 2, one of the five strands is 'Solving Problems', which identifies objectives for each year group under the headings 'Making decisions', 'Reasoning about numbers or shapes' and 'Solving problems involving "real life", money or measures'. At Key Stage 3 'Using and applying mathematics to solve problems' is one of the six strands.

- *Making and justifying decisions* about which method to use is a key element of the NNS's *approach to calculation*.

- At Key Stages 1 and 2, the *medium-term planning grids* include objectives from the 'Solving Problems' strand in nearly all the units of work and (in theory) about one week in each term is unallocated, some days of which could be used for more extended investigations.

- At Key Stage 3, the planning guidance recommends *integrating UAM* throughout.

- At Key Stage 3, *reasoning* (proportional, algebraic and geometric) and the concept of *proof* are distinctive elements.

- The *handling data cycle* is a similar process to the TASC Wheel.

Teaching strategies

Read the *Framework for Teaching Mathematics from Reception to Year 6* (DfEE 1999c), Section 1, pp. 11–15 and the *Framework for Teaching Mathematics: Years 7, 8 and 9* (DfEE 2001), Section1, pp. 26–27.

Consider links with the TASC thinking skills approach.

- Are we giving sufficient emphasis to:
  - teaching styles which will promote thinking skills?
  - objectives from the solving problems strand and other objectives relating to UAM in our planning and teaching, or are we mostly concerned with teaching content?

- How do our current medium-term plans incorporate these objectives? Are they 'tagged on' at the end of each unit of work? Could we do more to promote links between objectives within units?

- Are we including opportunities for a variety of investigative and problem-solving activities, within single lessons or extended over two or more lessons?

- Would the TASC approach provide a useful structure for these lessons?

- Could we put together a bank of ideas for investigative activities that link with different mathematical topics?

- Are there opportunities for cross-curricular links?

Note

The mathematics projects were carried out at: Cherry Orchard Primary School, Worcester; Hallow CE Primary School, Worcester; and Northwick Manor Junior School, Worcester.

Using TASC to Foster the Development of Problem-solving and Thinking Skills in Science

**STEVE DAVIES, RASHU ROSSO
and LUCY BELL-SCOTT**

I Want to Know

    – How flowers form – And why moons dawn
    – Why stars are bright – And fireflies light
    – Why people talk – But parrots squawk
    – Evolution? – Why pollution?
    – How fusion starts – And fission parts
    – Interplanetary? – Extraordinary?
    – How birds can fly – So why can't I?
    – How I can think – Sense or instinct?
    – And who am I? – To live and die?
              I Want to Know, Sam (age 11)

Introduction

Many science teachers around the country would read the above poem
and say 'But we are helping pupils to answer questions like these all
the time!' The DfEE/QCA Schemes of Work for Science (2000) refer
to the need to develop systematically pupils' skills of 'knowing why'
and 'how' as well as 'knowing what' in the development of their skills
of 'learning how to learn'. In each unit there are suggestions that
refer to the need for pupils to reflect on 'what', 'how' and 'why' they
have learned, and how they could extend their knowledge and skills.

Some of the thinking skills that are outlined as learning objectives include the following:

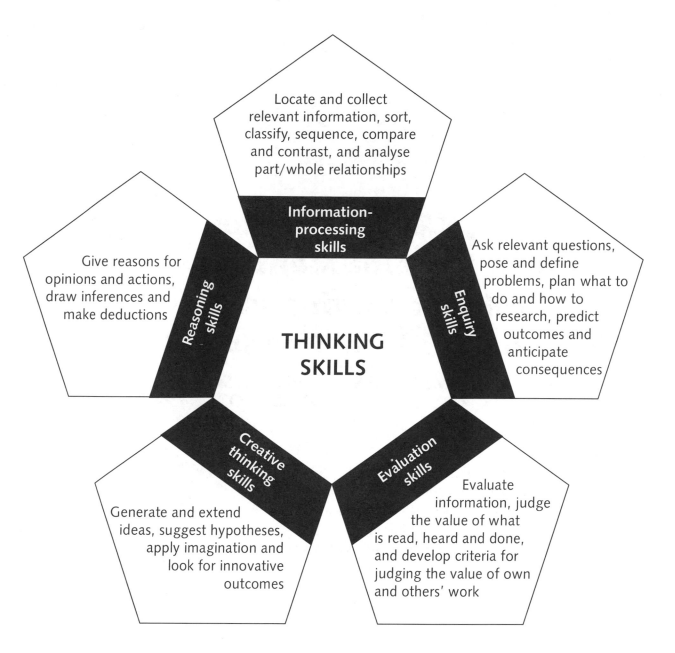

THINKING SKILLS

Information-processing skills — Locate and collect relevant information, sort, classify, sequence, compare and contrast, and analyse part/whole relationships

Enquiry skills — Ask relevant questions, pose and define problems, plan what to do and how to research, predict outcomes and anticipate consequences

Evaluation skills — Evaluate information, judge the value of what is read, heard and done, and develop criteria for judging the value of own and others' work

Creative thinking skills — Generate and extend ideas, suggest hypotheses, apply imagination and look for innovative outcomes

Reasoning skills — Give reasons for opinions and actions, draw inferences and make deductions

PURPOSE

The following two sections of this chapter explore how teachers, using the TASC Wheel and the Tools for Effective Thinking, can develop and consolidate the thinking skills outlined above.

Section 1 takes the topic 'Investigating materials and their properties: acids and bases', exploring it as a problem-solving exercise at Key Stage 3.

Section 2 takes the topic 'Investigating habitats' and develops it as a problem-solving exercise at Key Stage 2.

Section 1: Investigating Materials and their Properties: Acids and Bases, Key Stage 3

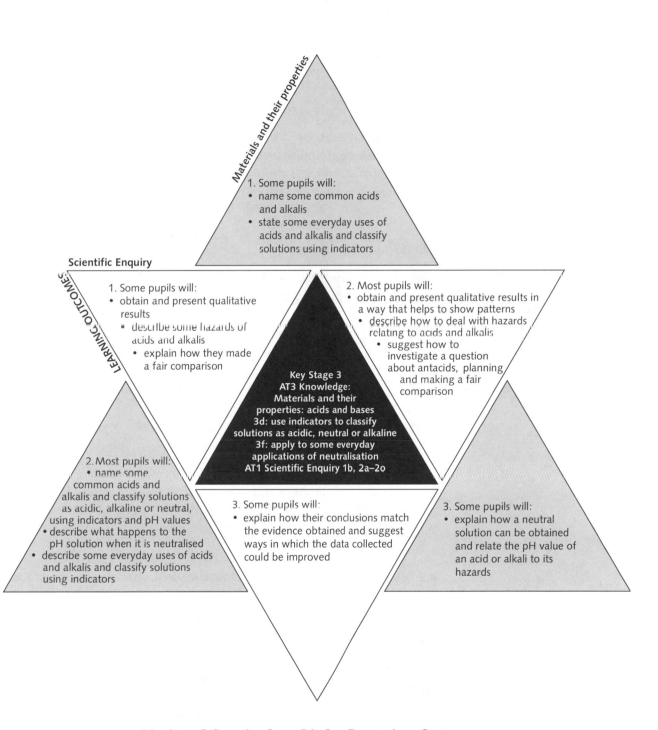

Materials and their properties

1. Some pupils will:
- name some common acids and alkalis
- state some everyday uses of acids and alkalis and classify solutions using indicators

Scientific Enquiry

1. Some pupils will:
- obtain and present qualitative results
- describe some hazards of acids and alkalis
- explain how they made a fair comparison

2. Most pupils will:
- obtain and present qualitative results in a way that helps to show patterns
- describe how to deal with hazards relating to acids and alkalis
- suggest how to investigate a question about antacids, planning and making a fair comparison

LEARNING OUTCOMES

Key Stage 3
AT3 Knowledge: Materials and their properties: acids and bases
3d: use indicators to classify solutions as acidic, neutral or alkaline
3f: apply to some everyday applications of neutralisation
AT1 Scientific Enquiry 1b, 2a–2o

2. Most pupils will:
- name some common acids and alkalis and classify solutions as acidic, alkaline or neutral, using indicators and pH values
- describe what happens to the pH solution when it is neutralised
- describe some everyday uses of acids and alkalis and classify solutions using indicators

3. Some pupils will:
- explain how their conclusions match the evidence obtained and suggest ways in which the data collected could be improved

3. Some pupils will:
- explain how a neutral solution can be obtained and relate the pH value of an acid or alkali to its hazards

National Curriculum Links: Learning Outcomes

Implementing the TASC Wheel

As the Science Coordinator at a middle school, the first time I saw the TASC Wheel I immediately thought — INVESTIGATIONS! The TASC Wheel would provide the pupils with a coherent and easy to follow framework for their investigations and would establish a pattern of working that should underpin all scientific investigation. The TASC Wheel would scaffold their learning, emphasising stages in problem-solving that are easily overlooked in the enthusiastic, and sometimes impulsive, 'doing' of the practical work.

I also realised that the TASC Wheel was a very useful framework for my own planning and this meant that I could more easily anticipate the learners' needs and their possible questions as well as crystallising in my mind the key learning objectives I was working towards.

The Wheel in motion!

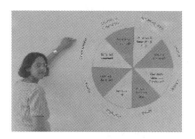

I decided to introduce the TASC Problem-solving Wheel at the outset and I enlarged and laminated the Wheel and pinned it up on the wall of the laboratory. We discussed why the TASC Wheel would help us to think and solve problems when we did our investigations, and the class conclusion was that it gave us an overall framework for our thinking and planning. The pupils could easily understand why the reflective stage of 'What have we learned?' was so important, and this discussion reinforced the idea that for all of us, our mistakes are our key learning points, and we always need to crystallise 'what' and 'how' and 'why' we learned.

The class then decided that we needed another wheel! The second wheel would complement the first TASC Problem-solving Wheel and remind us of the specific things we needed to think about in science. We would call our wheel 'Our Tools for Effective Thinking in Science'.

The Tools for Effective Thinking wheel consists of the ' science thinking tools' that the pupils considered the most important for a science investigation.

Our Tools for Effective Thinking in Science

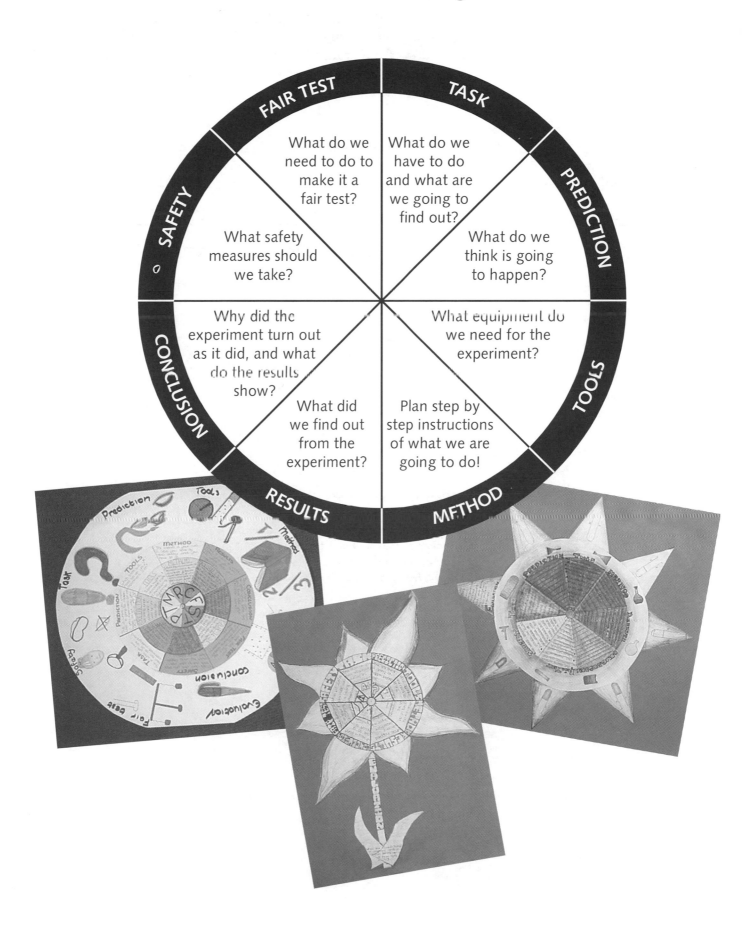

The investigation!

The main TASC Problem-solving Wheel was on the wall in the laboratory and could easily be read by all the pupils: this was our overall thinking framework. Then each pupil had a copy of the Our Tools for Effective Thinking in Science wheel, which was the immediate planning sheet.

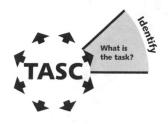

I decided to give the pupils the task by handing out a formal letter from a 'pharmaceutical company' which gave clear instructions (and a clue or two), and this created great enthusiasm.

RENNY-CO HEALTHCARE
YOUR WELFARE IS OUR CONCERN

FAX TO: *Analysts*
FROM: *Tom Acher*

The company wishes to test three stomach powders, A, B and C, to see if they neutralise stomach acid.

Please carry out some tests to tell me how much of each powder you need to neutralise the stomach acid. Make sure you do fair tests. Be as accurate as possible.

Our first tests show that one powder will not work at all.

Please investigate and compile a report on:
(1) how you carried out the tests
(2) your results
(3) which powder is most effective at neutralising stomach acid.

URGENT!

Thanks!

Tom

The class pooled all the information they already knew in the mindmap opposite.

Alkalis are chemical opposites to acids

When an acid is added to an alkali, it lowers the pH and vice versa

Neutral solutions have a pH of 7

A neutral solution is halfway between acid and alkali

pH numbers indicate how acidic or alkaline a solution is using a colour chart

NEUTRALISATION

Litmus goes red in acids and blue in alkalis

Acids and alkalis can change the colour of certain dyes and this can be used to classify them

We use some alkalis at home: baking powder, some tap water (chalky areas), some cleaning fluids, ammonia, garden lime

We can identify acids and alkalis with a substance which is called an indicator which changes colour

Universal indicator gives a range of colours in acidic and alkaline solutions

We use some acids at home: vinegar, lemon juice, coca-cola, aspirin, beer

We can identify alkalis with universal indicator (turns ——)

Many household materials are acids and they are not always hazardous

The pupils had their Tools for Effective Thinking in Science wheel and they completed their draft plans for the investigation. The wheel format enabled me to see the progress of all pupils. I could see the pupils who were quickly ready to begin the investigation and give help to those who got stuck at any point.

TASC

Which is the best idea?

Decide

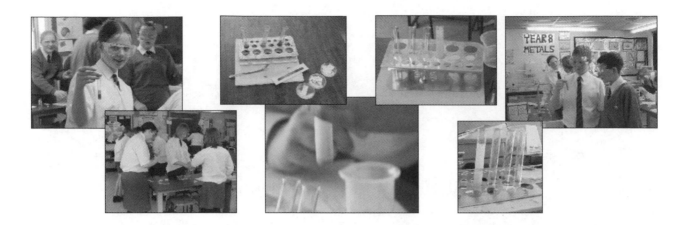

TASC

How well did I do?

Evaluate

The pupils used their planning notes from Our Tools for Effective Thinking in Science to evaluate how well they had worked. Having the sections in the wheel made it easier for pupils to consider each stage of their planning. Here are some of the pupils' comments:

We didn't notice that the pharmaceutical company gave us a clue when they said that one powder didn't work at all.

Sometimes you can't predict, you just have to do a series of tests.

We did a fair test because we measured the amount of powder and acid each time.

We worked safely because we were careful with the acid and the glassware.

Our plan helped us to work quickly because we did things in the right order.

We were careful to record our results accurately.

We could have weighed the amount of powder and this would have been more accurate.

We didn't think through the 'Prediction' carefully, we just guessed.

The pupils prepared a display and a series of flow charts to explain their fndings.

We used the TASC Problem-solving Wheel to focus in on the final overall reflection on what we had learned from the whole exercise. Here are some of the pupils' comments.

Doing experiments with the TASC Wheel is good training for your brain.

I think real scientists use the TASC Wheel automatically.

I am learning to think more clearly using the TASC Problem-solving framework.

The Science wheel is much more interesting than your average A4 layout.

The TASC Problem-solving Wheel helps you to think more logically.

Using a colour scheme for the segments, I can remember.

We can remember better because we think in sections first, then put it all together.

I feel more organised – I can work on specific sections in the Science wheel if I'm not sure about them.

We could do our own thinking because we made our own guidelines and the teacher didn't have to tell us everything.

What I have learned as a teacher

- The pupils took ownership of the original TASC Wheel, recognising the sense of it, and then they took great pride in creating Our Tools for Effective Thinking in Science. They were able to 'customise' the generic TASC Problem-solving Wheel to suit the purpose of a science investigation in the laboratory. I was surprised by their enthusiasm and their creativity.

- The practical work was very efficient since the pupils had thought everything through beforehand, and they were building patterns of effective classroom behaviour as well as good processes of scientific thinking. It was the most independent task the pupils had carried out and their confidence level was very high.

- Differentiation was easy to build into the Science wheel since pupils could proceed at their own rate and I had time to support those who needed help. Assessment of the pupils' work was much easier since I could monitor and moderate the whole investigative task by referring to the pupils' planning and recording as they worked. I could also focus on any particular segment in the Science wheel that seemed to be causing problems.

- The pupils were able to go beyond the information given, to deal systematically yet flexibly with the problems they encountered, to adopt a critical attitude to the information given and to communicate their ideas freely.

- The more able pupils wheeled their way through the TASC Wheel and the Science wheel: they revelled in both the organisational structure and also the autonomy and freedom both wheels provided.

- I built in the important TASC reflective stage when all the investigative work had been completed, and we could discuss how we had worked in a team, what we had learned about the work of a science analyst, and what we needed to do to improve our performance for next time.

In conclusion, I have decided to work in the TASC way for at least one investigative project per science topic. It is easy to see how this way of working leads the pupils towards greater autonomy and independence.

Teachers from other departments have also approached me after seeing the display of the pupils' work. They have asked if they can adjust the TASC Problem-solving Wheel for use in their subject area and this has led me to consider the possibility of delivering INSET to the whole staff. This could lead to the TASC Problem-solving Wheel being used as a whole-school approach, and I am certain that we could raise the levels of confidence, independence and achievement of all our pupils.

Section 2: Investigating Habitats (Key Stage 2)

The following chart indicates the sections that were developed from
the National Curriculum Guidelines for Science.

Overall planning within which the TASC project was located

		Weekly/Mid-term plans		

Subject and lesson titles: Science and habitats

Context of lessons: To allow the pupils to learn about habitats and how the organisms live within them. To use investigation and research to discover and find out more about the locality of the school and the habitats within it.

National Curriculum requirements: SC1: 1a–b, 2a–m; SC2: 1a, 4a–c, 5a–e

Intended learning outcomes: To be able to identify some local habitats and the organisms that live in them. To make use of simple keys. To be able to state the food source of some organisms: herbivores and carnivores. To carry out an investigation to show that certain organisms prefer certain habitats.

	Week 1	Week 2	Week 3	Week 4
Lesson activities	Find out what the pupils know Define 'habitat' Investigate and record habitats around school Briefly describe each habitat Refer to video on habitats	Consolidate previous lesson Discuss and record Derive understanding of 'ecosystem'	Watch and discuss video Group a range of organisms Discuss rationale Create a key	Plan, predict and carry out investigation into why certain organisms are found in specific habitats Sharing of ideas
Learning objectives	Define habitat Recognise common habitats Understand 'ecosystem'	To understand concept of 'ecosystem' To collect and analyse evidence	To group common organisms To identify features	To derive and support hypotheses To predict outcome To investigate hypotheses
Teaching and management	Instruct and question Discuss observations Develop framework for observation and recording	Attend to different learning needs Oversee safe collection of animals for investigation	Discuss video Derive criteria for grouping organisms	Discuss video Derive investigation questions Plan investigations
Assessment	Discussion to consolidate and inform further lessons Identify needs for differentiation and support	Observation of pupils' progress	Based on progress of pupils	Record findings Present findings Formal assessment
Differentiation	Use classroom assistant appropriately Develop support within mixed ability groups	Match complex habitats with more able pupils, simpler habitats with the less able	Graduated activity sheet	Guide reading research Derive more complex investigation
Extra resources	Recording sheet Digital camera Video: Stage 2 Science (Channel 4)	Clipboards Recording sheets Collecting equipment Digital camera	Video: Stage 2 Science (Channel 4)	Collecting/sampling equipment

Note – Extension of the topic: Discuss and derive food chains; Discuss important issues in conservation of habitats; Design posters to 'Preserve Habitats'.

 **COMMENT** ▶

Our school is a small, one-form entry primary school where we have started to introduce the QCA Scheme of Work as the backbone to our work in science. Although we already actively develop practical and investigative work, I decided to use the TASC Wheel as a firm and holistic framework for the whole class of 29 pupils for their investigation of habitats. I decide to combine the two stages 'Generating an idea' and 'Deciding' and discussed the framework of the TASC Wheel with the pupils beforehand. We discussed how 'real' scientists work and referred to the TASC Wheel; the pupils were very excited at the thought of doing 'real investigative work' following the TASC procedure.

The children had been introduced to the topic of habitats in the week beforehand and had explored the range of habitats around the school. Therefore, when they divided into small groups, every child had a lot to contribute. They also used the digital photographs that they had taken as reminders of their observations.

What do we already know about habitats?

Gather/organise

What do I know about this?

TASC

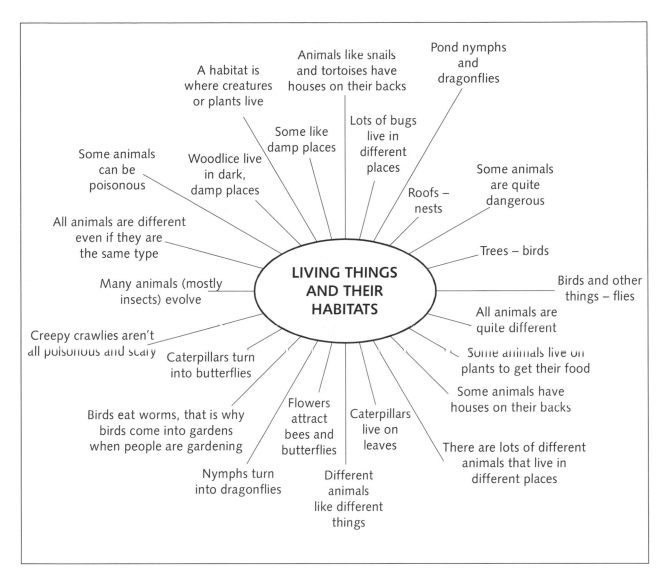

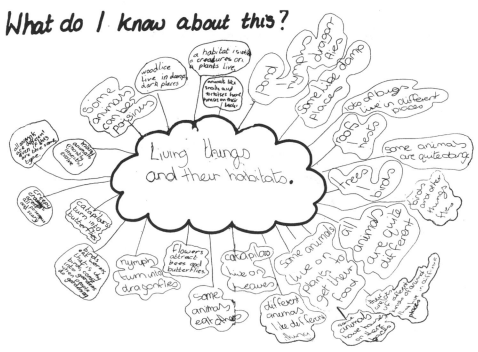

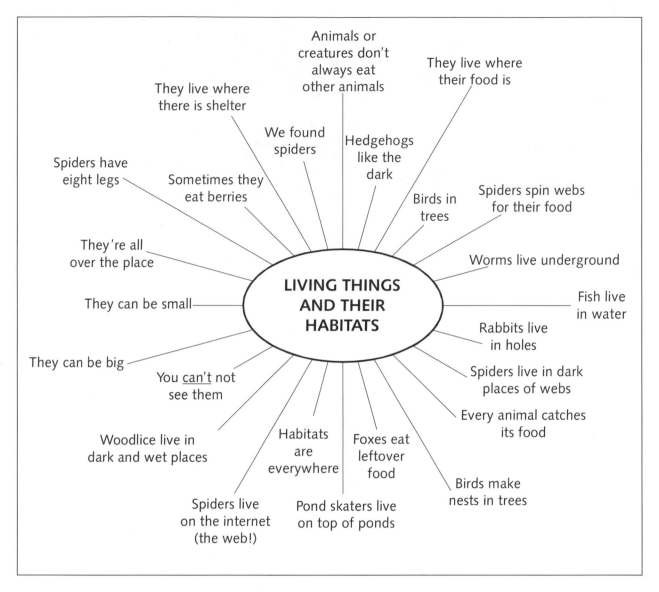

Animals or creatures don't always eat other animals

They live where their food is

They live where there is shelter

We found spiders

Hedgehogs like the dark

Spiders have eight legs

Sometimes they eat berries

Birds in trees

Spiders spin webs for their food

They're all over the place

Worms live underground

LIVING THINGS AND THEIR HABITATS

Fish live in water

They can be small

Rabbits live in holes

They can be big

Spiders live in dark places of webs

You can't not see them

Every animal catches its food

Woodlice live in dark and wet places

Habitats are everywhere

Foxes eat leftover food

Birds make nests in trees

Spiders live on the internet (the web!)

Pond skaters live on top of ponds

In order to take the children further in their investigation of habitats, we generated a range of interesting questions that we could explore. The pupils were keen and enthusiastic, and although some of the questions were beyond the scope we could explore in school, we decided that we would investigate whether insects could make choices as to where they preferred to live, or what they preferred to eat.

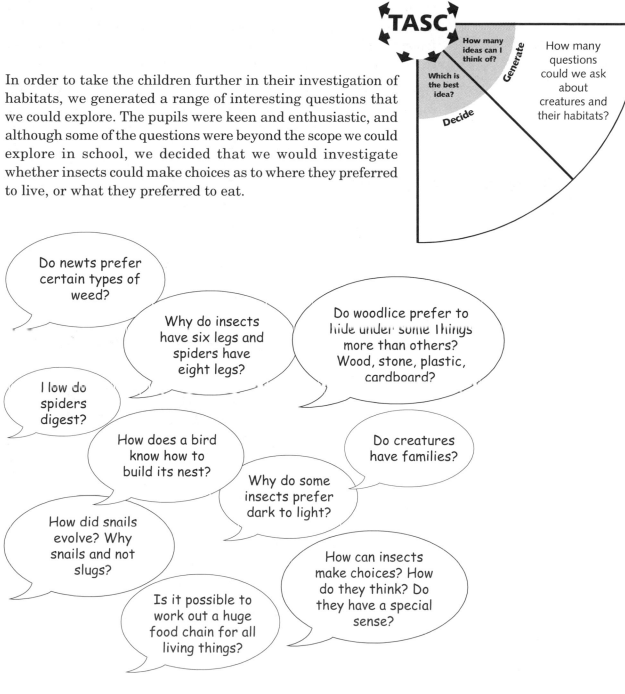

Having decided that we would investigate whether insects could make choices, we again generated questions about how to make 'choice chambers'.

Ideas flooded out! Some pupils converted cardboard boxes into rooms, some constructed a series of tunnels, and one group considered setting up playrooms and toilets! The pupils worked in groups to draw plans of how to make their choice chambers and how to care for their creatures: then they listed the apparatus they needed. Results were recorded using a variety of methods – tables, photographs and diagrams – with one group strictly recording at timed intervals. The following photographs and diagrams give examples of the range of choice chambers that were made.

Here is a choice chamber for centipedes: both sides were identically constructed with a small tunnel connecting the two. One side was dry and the other side damp.

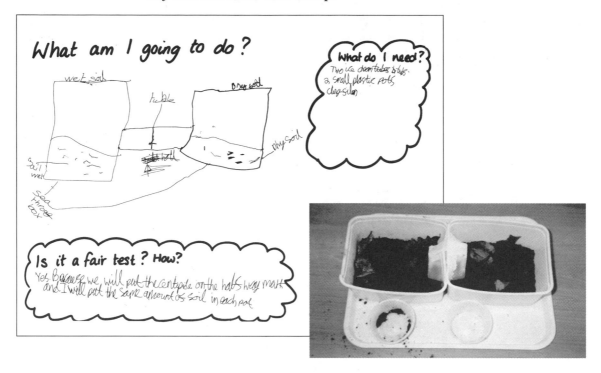

This is a worm investigation: equal numbers of worms were put into 3 jars with layers of soil and sand prepared with different conditions: dark, light and wet. The more the worms liked the conditions, the more the active they were in mixing the layers.

This shows the planning and conclusion for a worm choice chamber that investigated conditions of light and dark.

The pupils prepared a presentation of their investigations to share with the rest of the class. They reported on what they had wanted to find out, how well their choice chambers had worked, and what they had learned. Some pupils had already formulated their next experiment to extend their knowledge and they were eager to continue their investigation in their own time over the half-term holiday.

When you work as a scientist, you need to be good at noticing things.

Using the TASC Wheel helped me to plan clearly.

We could use the TASC Wheel in all our subjects.

The TASC Wheel guides you and you don't have to ask the teacher what to do.

I really enjoyed planning my own investigation.

Mindmaps help you to think.

I remembered things I thought I had forgotten.

I learned how to plan my own experiment.

I now know how to design my own investigation, and I'm going to do this in the holidays.

When we gathered and organised what we already knew, I learned a lot from the other kids.

Nymphs and Newts

A **diary** was kept describing movements of both creatures in the water tank. The results showed little movement of the nymphs, which stayed in the pond weed. The newts, by contrast, moved in and out of the light and were very active. On returning the creatures to the pond, the same pattern was observed. The children wanted to investigate further by considering if the water temperature affected their movement. This investigation was reported back to the whole class **verbally**.

Worms – do worms prefer wet or dry?

The results of observations were recorded **pictorially**. The worms were placed in the middle area with a wet area to one side and a dry area to the other side. Two observations were made in one day. Lines made by the worms were counted and examined. The children decided, on this basis, which area the worms preferred.

Worms – do worms prefer light or dark?

A **table** was drawn up to record each morning, for one week, where the worms were.

Spiders – do spiders prefer the light or the dark?

Using a colour code to identify the three different spiders, a **record** was made of where they chose to be at three different times in the day. The results showed a preference for the dark.

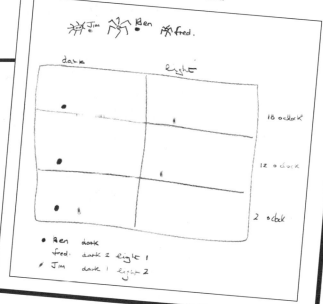

COMMENT

The children were engrossed in their investigations right from the beginning, and my role was that of questioner and facilitator. Some of the experiments were rather too ambitious at the outset, but through discussion the pupils were able to modify their investigations to something manageable. The apparatus was simple – large jars, boxes, card, cling-film and Sellotape – but the children were very inventive and flexible within these constraints.

In the presentations, the pupils were confident and everyone contributed; even the usually shy, more reticent pupils had a lot to say about what they had learned. Importantly, the pupils who were generally reluctant to record were eager to share their ideas, enjoying the oral emphasis but willing to produce sufficient written work to communicate their ideas and conclusions.

My reflections

● I needed to be sure what I wanted the children to learn so that my questioning was clearly directed towards the learning objective.

● The pupils took ownership of their investigations and needed no prompting to remain 'on task'.

● I was working towards literacy and ICT objectives in the final presentation of the pupils' work.

● My organisation needed to be flexible in order to accommodate the different kinds of investigations the children wanted to pursue.

● The children kept rough notes until they needed to work towards their presentation, so that they gave maximum attention to 'thinking' and minimum attention to the neatness of the recording.

● The TASC framework gave the pupils the necessary scaffolding for their own enquiry-based learning and I saw them grow as independent learners. Since then, they have wanted to work in the TASC way whenever there was an opportunity to do so.

Note

The 'Acids and Bases' Project was carried out at Aston Fields Middle School, Worcs. The 'Habitats' Project was carried out at Whittington C/E Primary School, Worcs.

Using ICT to Support the Development of Problem-solving and Thinking Skills

6

JANE FINCH

Information and communication technology (ICT) offers new opportunities to teach for creativity through new forms of creative practice . . . and new ways of working with traditional forms . . . It can revolutionise teaching and learning through easier and greater access to information, ideas, and people. (National Campaign for the Arts 2000)

Introduction

Consider the potential of ICT in supporting the development of thinking skills:

- What is the potential contribution of ICT to the establishment and development of an appropriate 'thinking climate' or environment?

- What is it about the computer that might be seen to be significant in this respect?

ICT is a powerful tool which can provide a variety of environments that stimulate and promote the development of problem-solving and thinking skills; it is the use of this tool, and not the subject itself, that is our focus here.

The computer:

● is non-judgemental;

● requires the user to take control in order to achieve the desired outcome;

● does not anticipate what the user is going to do;

● has infinite 'patience';

● will give pupils all the thinking time they need.

ICT provides environments in which particular types of problem-solving are required and assists with the solving of problems. The TASC problem-solving model provides an ideal framework against which to develop challenging programmes.

REFLECT

Do you agree?

● Are there any 'qualities' you would wish to add? Or to qualify?

● In considering the role of ICT, is there an important distinction to be made between ICT *activity* and ICT *capability*?

COMMENT

ICT activity	**ICT capability**
is characterised by the *interaction of the pupil with the computer* through a piece of software. It is often the activity that becomes the focus, e.g. the creation of a desktop-published document or the development of a spreadsheet model.	is characterised by the *use of the technology to solve a particular problem*. Clearly pupils need to know a range of techniques in order to do so, but the key to ICT capability is the application of techniques and key ideas for a particular purpose.
In fact, it is actually the thinking *which goes on around the activity that is the most important factor for higher attainment.*	*This requires* higher-order thinking skills *in order for the pupils to go beyond the obvious solution and to look for innovative routes through a problem.*

This chapter explores two examples of classroom activity in the middle years in which ICT is used to support students as they strive to solve a complex problem. These are summarised as follows:

PURPOSE

Section A: Combining drama and ICT	Section B: Using ICT to facilitate mindmapping
'ICT and drama' deals with a cross-curricular project in which ICT was incidental but important as a communication tool. Thinking about how you communicate effectively with different groups of people using different methods was central to the activity . . . ICT provided some of the means through video, audio tape, DTP, e-mail and graphics.	The use of ICT to aid the development of ideas and to structure thinking has been made easier by the development of mindmapping software. Unlike a pencil-drawn concept map, the software allows the user to reorganise the diagram and look at it in a variety of ways at the click of a button.

WebQuests* are an example of a scaffolded learning structure and are based on the use of the TASC Problem-solving Wheel (see pp. 131ff.).

The chapter sets out to demonstrate aspects of the ICT contribution to a thinking environment, and of the interrelationship between capability and activity.

In addition, it shows how the medium of ICT supports the development of thinking skills as it allows pupils to change their minds readily as their thinking around an activity develops. They are not inhibited from having further 'good ideas' by the knowledge that this will simply generate the need to rewrite their response.

It also shows that ICT facilitates the use of layered models of organising concepts, ideas and thinking. It provides pupils with flexible ways of communicating their ideas in a wide variety of forms.

Finally, the TASC framework for the teaching of problem-solving and thinking skills provides an essential range of skills and strategies that need to be systematically embedded in any programme purporting to develop thinking skills.

Section A: Combining drama and ICT

Investigating, reporting and making judgement on a theft

● PURPOSE

This section deals with a cross-curricular project in which ICT supports the investigation and communication of the events surrounding the 'real' trial of an alleged thief. Thinking about how you communicate effectively with different groups of people using different methods was central to the activity. ICT provided some of the means through video, audio tape, DTP, e-mail and graphics.

During the activity pupils are given the opportunity to practise:

- sorting and evaluating evidence

- considering the arguments for and against

- using evidence to make and justify a decision

- role play and empathising: being able to see an issue from the point of view of another person

- communicating

COMMENT ▶

This day-long workshop used a drama student to play the leading character in the scenario that was to unfold. Using a role player always adds a dimension to any drama work, as pupils have a dynamic, central focus on which to base all their interactions. The workshop was run on eight occasions, with different groups of mixed ability pupils from the middle years. This article combines experiences from all of them.

The activity required students to investigate and role play the 'real' trial of an alleged thief, a young woman who was accused of stealing money from a purse in a gift shop.

Overall planning and discussion using the TASC Wheel

The pupils were introduced to the TASC Problem-solving Wheel, as shown in the centre of the diagram below. They discussed how the TASC Wheel could guide their thinking and planning and, with suggestions to prompt their thinking, they derived a range of questions they felt they needed to consider in the course of their investigation.

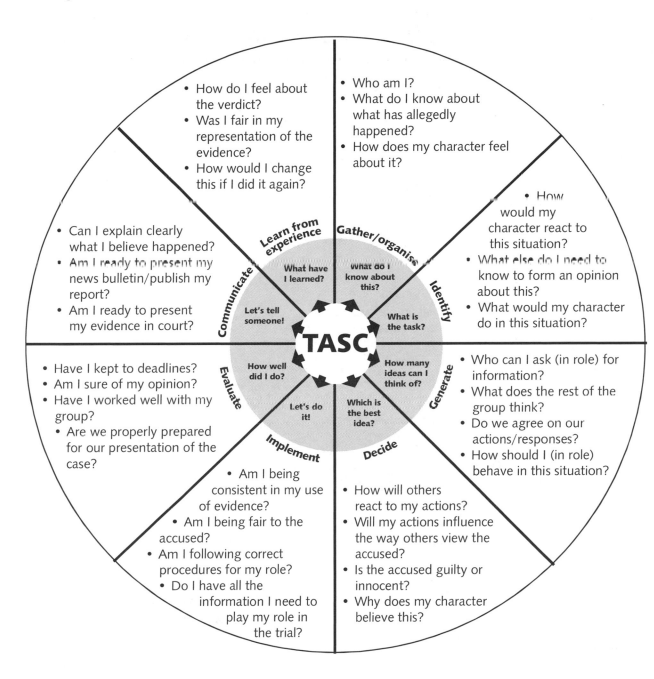

The range of Tools for Effective Thinking that evolved during the pupils' discussion as they identified the needs of the activity

The most important skill pupils could bring to the day was their ability to think in different ways. When presented with a vast array or a frustratingly limited range of evidence they had to make some sense of the story that was unfolding before them as dictated by their role.

The wide range of tools for effective thinking employed by various groups during the day are shown on the mindmap below.

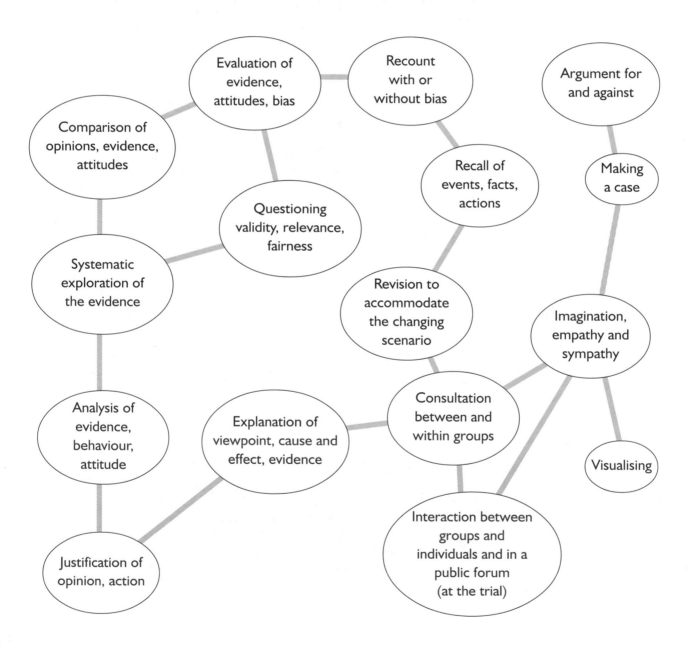

Tools for Effective Thinking

The range of ICT skill areas used during the investigation

Pupils were given access to ICT throughout the day and they were able to use computers, laptops, video and audio recording as needed. Some activities *required* the use of technology, but in others it was elective. The intention was to allow the use of technology (in its widest sense) to communicate as people do in real life.

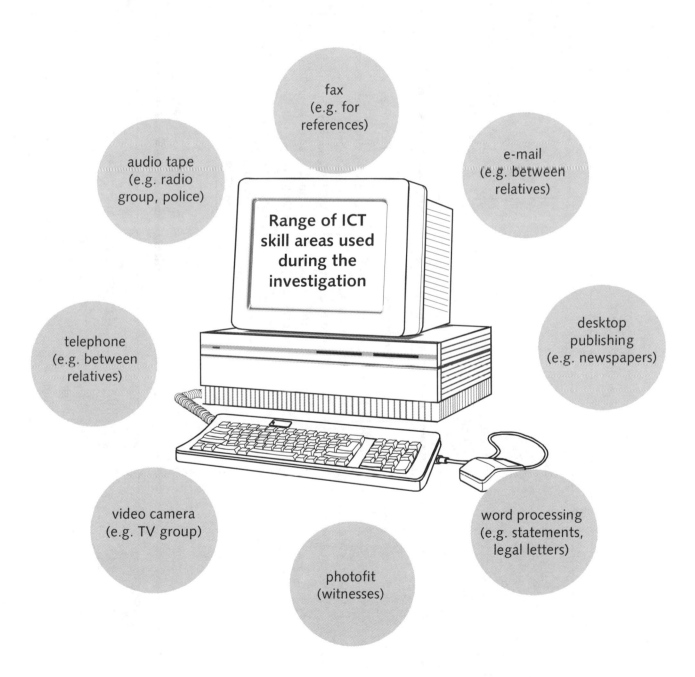

Outline plan of drama and ICT workshops for middle years pupils

- Children will work in groups to a fairly rigid timetable.
- The accused will be played by a role player who will determine, on the day, whether she is guilty or not.
- The stimulus will be footage of security video, showing the offender was present at the scene of the 'crime'.

INCIDENT (stimulus)

Video using actual security camera footage with offender in it.

Only to be shown to witnesses, defence lawyers and police

Accused (role player)

- Make statement, provide alibi, etc.
- Talk to 'defence lawyer'
- Receive visit from relatives and/or friends
- Take part in trial

Reporters (three media groups)

- Interview observers
- Interview victim
- Interview relatives for background information

- Note-taking
- Use tape recorder
- Word process newspaper report
- Prepare sandwich board headline
- Video TV news bulletin/report

Relatives

- Offender's relatives' reactions to his/her behaviour
- Visit offender in prison (handling an awkward situation)
- Write letters to friends
- Make telephone calls to friends and family
- React to news reports

Witnesses

- Make statements to police
- Give interview to press
- Give evidence to court
- Write letters to friends
- Make phone calls to friends
- Make Photofit of offender

Police

- Interview accused
- Interview observers
- Interview victim
- Note-taking
- Use tape recorder
- Photofit using MyWorld2–FaceIT
- Word process report on incident

Lawyers (two groups)

- Conduct interviews
- Write notes ready for hearing
- Interrogate witnesses at the trial

TRIAL (conclusion of the day's activities)

- Role play drawing together all strands of the activity
- Teacher to act as judge
- Each group to provide two members for jury (except defence and prosecution)

TV interview

The jury

Giving evidence

Police interview

The prosecution

Organisational planning showing roles, tasks and access to information

Time/Group	Relatives	Police	Prosecution	Defence	TV	Radio	Newspaper	Witnesses
Session 1	Family meeting with the accused	Watch security video	Read brief	Read brief	Practise using video recorder	Practise using tape recorder	Practise using software	Watch video once only
Session 2	Letters/e-mails to friends individually	Photofit with witnesses	See security video	Interview the accused	Prepare questions Listen to victim's taped interview	Prepare questions Listen to victim's taped interview	Prepare questions Listen to victim's taped interview	Photofit with police Make police statement
Session 3	Newspaper interview	Prepare questions	Interview the accused	Video/prepare questions	Press conference with relatives	Press conference with relatives	Press conference with relatives	Record radio interview
Session 4	TV/radio interviews	Take statement from the accused	Prepare questions	Interview witnesses	Write up notes Prepare questions	Write up notes Prepare questions	Write up notes Prepare questions	Interviewed by defence
Session 5	Police	Press conference	Interview witnesses	Prepare case	Police press conference	Police press conference	Police press conference	Interviewed by prosecution
Session 6	Watch/listen to TV/radio bulletin. Family conference	Interview witnesses	TV interview	Relatives	Midday bulletin	Midday bulletin	Make newspaper billboard	Listen/watch bulletins Give police statement
Lunch	Lunch	Lunch	Lunch	Lunch	Lunch	Lunch	Lunch	Lunch
Session 7	Record TV appearance	Investigation meeting	Interview any helpful relatives	TV interview	Complete report	Complete report	Prepare final copy	Prepare for trial. Use prompt sheets
Session 8	Record radio interview. Look at media presentations	Prepare case Decide who will present the police case in court	Prepare case Decide which witnesses to call	Prepare case Decide which witnesses to call	1.30pm full report	1.30pm full report	Afternoon edition available to read	See/hear TV/radio broadcasts. Read newspaper article
Session 9	Trial	Trial	Trial	Trial	Trial	Trial	Trial	Trial

 *General rules and procedures*

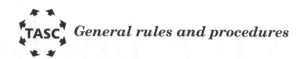 COMMENT ▶

A strict timetable was devised for the day so that each group could have the amount of time to interact with the role player and with other groups as necessary to build the whole picture of the incident.

Pupils were divided into eight groups of three or four, depending on class size. Each group was assigned a specific relationship to the role player, the *accused*.

Each group built its own version of the story based on the evidence and at the end of the day a judge and jury tried the *accused*.

Each group was given clear written guidance about their role within the drama, so part of the overall activity was pre-specified.

A mixture of sympathetic and unsympathetic roles was defined for the **Relations** group. They had no access to any of the evidence. Their version of events was provided by the *accused*.

Witnesses were shown the security video *once* and asked to place themselves in the shop and devise a scenario that included them in the story. Using the floor plan, they could identify where they might have been in the shop, what they might have purchased and what they might have seen. They also created a Photofit image of the **accused** on the computer.

The **Police** group was expected to take statements from **Witnesses** and the *accused*, give press briefings, provide information to the **Defence** and **Prosecution** and provide security at the trial.

The **Prosecution** and **Defence** groups were required to put together an appropriate argument to be presented at the trial. They each interviewed the *accused*, the **Police** and **Witnesses** and were allowed to call two people to give evidence at the trial.

The media groups had two deadlines to meet:

Deadline	Newspaper	Television	Radio
Lunchtime	Create a billboard headline which will provide the basis for an article	Create a short bulletin to camera giving the outline of events	Record a short news bulletin giving the outline of events
End of the day	Using a DTP package produce a full report of the crime in newspaper style, including appropriate quotes. Bias it towards not guilty or guilty	Create a news bulletin to camera including interviews and an outline of events surrounding the crime. Bias it towards not guilty or guilty	Record a full news bulletin including interviews and an outline of events surrounding the crime. Bias it towards not guilty or guilty

Students were guided to use the whole TASC Wheel to guide the creation of their finished products.

The media groups were allowed to interview anyone who would co-operate, as well as gather information from press conferences in order to put these together. They had no access to any evidence except the tape of the *victim*.

Using and presenting the evidence

The key piece of evidence was a piece of security video showing the *accused* in a gift shop. She clearly picked up a purse, which had been left on the counter by another customer, but the video did not show clearly whether she took anything from the purse.

The additional evidence supplied to various groups as appropriate included:

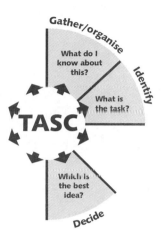

- statements from the shop keeper and the *victim* whose money was taken;

- a tape of an interview with the *victim* providing some more personal details about the effect of the loss;

- the purse;

- the hat allegedly worn by the *accused*;

- a character reference for the *accused* from a large supermarket;

- a financial reference for the *accused* from her bank;

- a floor plan of the shop.

The final part of the day was the **trial**, at which an adult took the part of the judge, but the pupils performed all other roles. Those pupils who were not required to give evidence, or who already had roles at the trial, drew lots to create a **jury**. The rest of the pupils occupied the public gallery. As far as possible, all correct procedures, including appropriate oaths and court etiquette, were observed during the trial and the pupils took it very seriously.

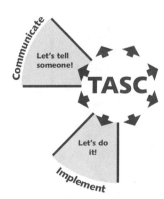

At the beginning of each workshop the *accused* decided whether she was guilty or innocent. *No one else knew.* She dressed in a particular style for the trial (which may have been very different from the way she had dressed for the rest of the day). On various occasions she was smart, trendy, casual or slovenly to try to influence the pupils' impressions of her during the trial.

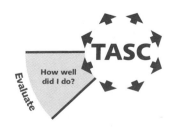

The **Witnesses** were generally very nervous about giving evidence: no scripts were allowed!

> I got nervous at the start but I found by the end of the day I wasn't worried at all. I think all the groups did very well, especially the defence lawyers. It felt like everything really happened because we were acting all day. I always wondered what it would be like to go to court and now I've got an idea of what it might be like.

> I liked the trial. I was longing to stand up and say, 'Your Honour, I object'. The only thing I would change is to try to make the atmosphere a bit better for The Court. [Written feedback from Amy, aged 10]

The **Prosecution** and **Defence** were equally nervous and there were some keenly contested battles between them. Winning the case became paramount.

The jury was required to achieve a majority verdict and was allowed a short time for discussion to achieve this. Each time a guilty verdict was returned the jurors expressed the difficulty they had experienced in making negative judgements about another person.

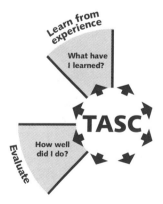

At the end of each day all pupils were debriefed to establish the learning that had taken place and to allow them to express their feelings about the different situations into which they had been placed. This was the only time when the whole group discussed the problem together and on occasions feelings ran high: members of the public gallery felt that their views had been misrepresented, witnesses felt intimidated, police felt overloaded, relatives felt cut out – *that's life!*

I felt annoyed sitting in the public gallery because Robert didn't say what we'd agreed . . . [Mark (**Witness**) on Robert's performance at the trial]

I was so nervous . . . it was difficult to remember when the Prosecution kept going on at me. [Robert (**Witness**)]

I think our group [Police] had more to do than the others . . . we had to collect all the statements and then give the press briefings . . . the Prosecution and Defence wanted to interview us. We had to work really hard all day. [Sally (**Police**)]

It didn't seem fair as we didn't see any of the evidence, like the other groups. All we could know was what Emma (the accused) told us – she changed her story twice. It was difficult to decide whether to believe her. [Chris (**Relatives**)]

Using the TASC Wheel helped me to sort out all the information . . . so it was quicker and easier to work. [Sally (**Police**)]

We had to work really hard to meet the deadlines. All the other groups were busy and didn't want to talk to us . . . but I enjoyed it! [William (**Media**)]

I learned that people see the same thing in different ways. [Tom (**Police**)]

I understand how difficult it is to be really fair when making a decision. [Hannah (**Lawyers**)]

I thought I knew who was guilty . . . then I listened to other people and thought about the evidence . . . I've learned not to jump to conclusions. [James (**Media**)]

Some examples of students' work at different stages of the process are shown overleaf.

Using a simple floor plan to build a picture of a character's inolvement at the scene of the crime

Novelty gifts and toys	Security camera
Books	Security camera
Computer games etc	
	Greetings cards
Ice cream fridge	Magazines
	Serving Counter

T shirts Caps etc

Postcards

Security camera

Pick 'n' mix sweets

Window

A personal perspective

Dear Tim,

Sharon is in lots of trouble and we will soon be on T.V radio and in the papers. We will look forward to hearing for you soon,
This is very serious I know. we all think she is gilty and we know she is.
She has gone and stole Mrs Willis's money out of her purse, which had £50 in there.
What Job do you have? do you still have that job near you. we are very well hear apart for this business. How is your family geting on, Inwhat way do you feel about Sharon, Doing this.
I wish to hear from you soon.

Yours Sincerely

Luke

What did we see?

wide brim hat

hat covering eyes

long black coat

I was standing at the pick and mix talking to a girl and I saw the victim leave her purse on the counter to collect some more gifts . Then an old man and woman went up to the counter the old man seemed to hide the lady but when they left the purse was untouched . After a while a different lady came up to the counter. She wore a black hat and she had tied back hair. She then picked up the purse and seemed to take some money out then she left .
Then the victim collected the empty purse and went.

Factual reporting?

The Sun
GUILTY OR NOT
by Mark Right

The crime took place at Coopers Gift Shop. Mrs WILLIS left her wallet on the side of the counter and did not realise what had happened but the shop keeper did not see it.
Later on a old couple came in and bought some sweets and left the shop the next person who came in was Sharon Woodhead .The accused Sharon picked up the wallet and opened it she said she was looking for a name but at the moment nobody knows.
Sharonn Woodheud has been let out on bail at the moment.
The last person in the shop was Sharon said the shopkeeper the police are not very sure.
Mrs Willis has three children and is on her own Mrs Willis is 45 she says it's not easy bringing up three children on her own.

The mother of the relatives says NO to the crime but the father says yes .
The father says yes because she is short of
money and spends it at the pub .
The mother says no because she is not that
kind of person .
The father of the family says she goes out a lot .
Sharon Woodheud the one who has been accused is still in

The police are not sure that Sharon did it police said the old couple did not do it and have nothing to do with it there was $50 or more taken .
The police have no details about the crime they say it could be Sharon the police have watched the video and are not sure .

Section B: Using ICT to facilitate mindmapping

To enable pupils to embark on an historical investigation and, at the same time, practise and develop mindmapping skills using Inspiration© and WebQuest.

Inspiration© is a software package that provides a visual learning environment. It integrates visual mapping and outlining to help pupils understand concepts and information. Pupils use Inspiration's Diagram view to create and modify mind or concept maps, idea maps, webs and other graphical organisers. Switching to the Outline view helps students quickly prioritise and rearrange ideas, helping them create clear, concise writing.

WebQuestUK provides a way of using Internet resources, alongside other resources within a clearly defined structure that scaffolds learning. There is always an opportunity to reconstruct knowledge in order to demonstrate transfer.

WebQuestUK develops the webquest concept in line with UK National Curriculum 2000. It enables students to work towards communicating their ideas about a *task* as the result of working through a clear *process* that provides a range of resources and guidance.

WebQuestUK uses the TASC Problem-solving Model to guide the structuring of the problems to be solved; Inspiration is a valuable tool in supporting this.

COMMENT

Inspiration© was given to middle years pupils who were embarking on an historical investigation through a WebQuest. Links from WebQuests to segments of the TASC Wheel provide questions to help pupils consider how they are working at each stage of their journey to a solution.

They had already had access to a suitcase of artefacts that belonged to a lady in 1908. From the articles in the suitcase they had made various deductions about the lady in question, such as her occupation and status, state of health and financial status.

They were asked to consider what might have happened to Edith Houghland given the following scenario:

> On the 28th of February 1908, a railway carriage door flew open before the train had come to a halt at Eastbourne Station. Edith Houghland tumbled out, struck her head on the platform, and died. The only thing that remained was her travelling case and her possessions inside.

The WebQuest provides a set of links to useful websites, but the first task was to use what we knew from the artefacts in the suitcase to build a picture of possible scenarios.

The TASC Wheel led naturally to the use of the software to establish possible scenarios. The way in which the first part of the TASC Wheel supported the investigation is shown in the diagram below. The combination of TASC and the software helped to find links between the various scenarios that the pupils developed.

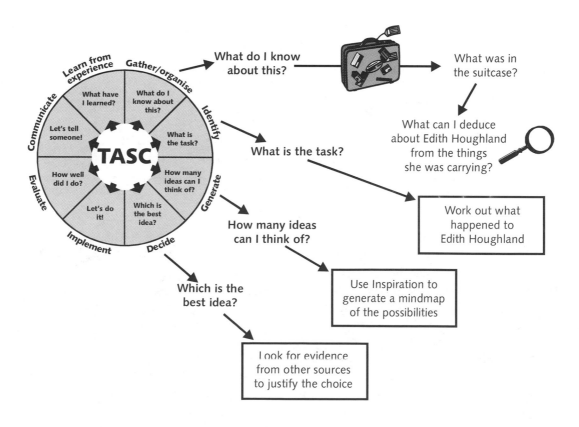

The initial mindmap was generated as a whole-class activity, with everybody contributing. The teacher acted as scribe using a laptop computer connected to a digital projector so that the whole class could see easily and had equal opportunity to contribute or edit the suggestions of others.

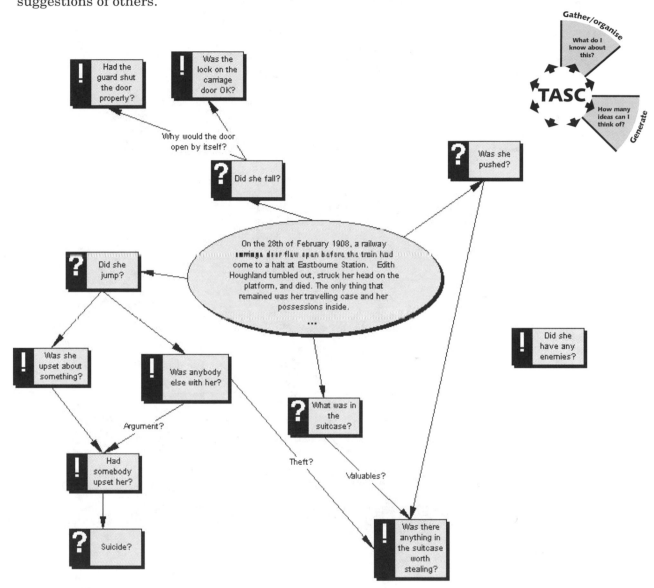

The initial map (above) was used by groups of pupils to develop their own ideas. One group in particular was becoming irritated by the complexity of their mindmap as they added more links and boxes.

They were shown the facility to convert their map to a top-down design and, with some manipulation of the elements making it up and the use of colour, they produced a model that was more meaningful to them (overleaf).

Each of the hypotheses was annotated by the pupils to expand their theories and at the end of the lesson there was a variety of well-reasoned suggestions about the fate of Edith Houghland.

Did she fall or was she pushed?

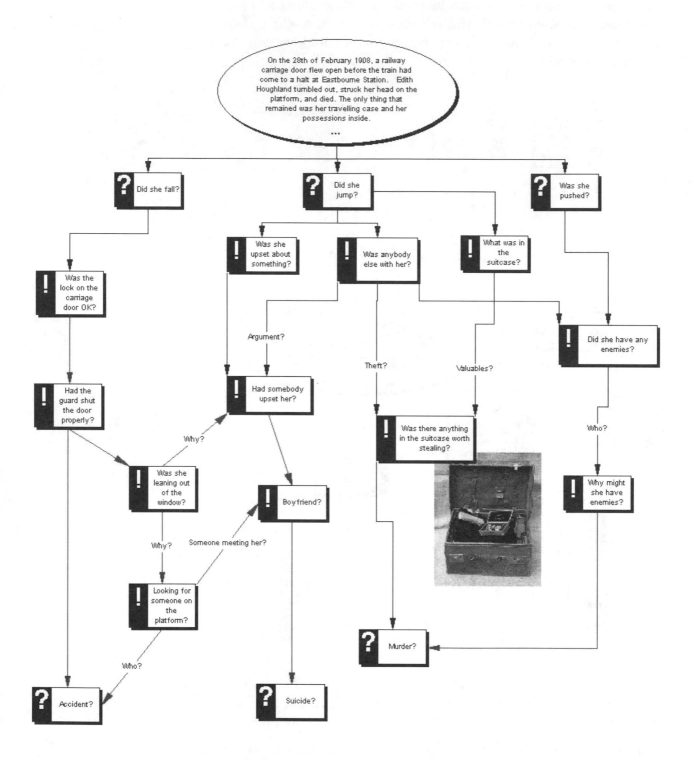

On the 28th of February 1908, a railway carriage door flew open before the train had come to a halt at Eastbourne Station. Edith Houghland tumbled out, struck her head on the platform, and died. The only thing that remained was her travelling case and her possessions inside.

...

? Did she fall?

? Did she jump?

? Was she pushed?

! Was the lock on the carriage door OK?

! Was she upset about something?

! Was anybody else with her?

! What was in the suitcase?

! Had the guard shut the door properly?

Argument?

Theft?

Valuables?

! Did she have any enemies?

! Had somebody upset her?

Why?

! Was she leaning out of the window?

! Boyfriend?

! Was there anything in the suitcase worth stealing?

Who?

! Why might she have enemies?

Why?

Someone meeting her?

! Looking for someone on the platform?

Who?

? Accident?

? Suicide?

? Murder?

http://learning.worcestershire.gov.uk/webquests/Completed%20Quests/Houghland%202/index.htm
Investigation plan produced on Inspirations6 (©Inspiration Software Inc.)
UK version suppliers: TAG Developments Ltd, 25 Pelham Road, Gravesend, Kent DA11 0HU, Tel. 01474 357350

Maybe she was pushed off the train by someone who wanted the medicine for themselves or to sell to other people.

She was a thief, but a good one.

She might have been a nurse because she had all sorts of medicines in her suitcase. So we think she looked after rich old people and when they died she took their leftover medicines and used them to help poor people get better.

When we started I thought it was just an accident. The door wasn't shut properly. As the train jolted she knocked against it and it opened.

So it was an accident.

She had asthma . . . that's why she had those things in the case.

But I've been talking to the others and now I don't know. She could be murdered. I hope it was an accident. Does anybody know for real what happened?

She might have had a bad attack and fallen out of the door . . .

Conclusion

Both the scenarios for problem-solving outlined above can be replicated using any data drawn from real life, history, geography, environmental science or the emerging curriculum topic of citizenship.

Students need access to relevant information, through which they systematically practise the use of the TASC Wheel, appropriate Tools for Effective Thinking and a range of ICT materials and skills.

The following flowcharts show the planning for two projects in history which combine the TASC Problem-solving Model and relevant ICT tools to create the finished product.

Outline of an extension project based on the history topic: 'Britain since 1930'

Pupils used their ICT skills to record and refine their ideas and to create their final product.

History skills: 2, 3, 4a/b
Literacy skills: 2a/c, 5a/c, 8a
Speaking and listening skills: 3a/b/c/d/f
Reading skills: 2a/c/d, 4a/b/c/d, 8b

The TASC Wheel gives you a plan to work to. It helps you to get work done

Using ICT means you can revise and make changes easily

If we write in the style of another author, we know how to plan

We learned how to plan and revise like a real writer

We now know how to go about an analysis of an author

We feel we communicated and worked well together

- Read to other classes
- Perform a play
- Illustrate and bind the book

Learn from experience
What have I learned?
Communicate
Let's tell someone!
How well did I do?
Evaluate
Let's do it!
Implement
TA

Write the story.
- Does it flow?
  - Is it exciting?
    - Have we kept to the style?
      - Are the characters real?
        - Is the language appropriate?

Further extension

Interview someone who was a child in the 1950s and compare their life with yours.

1950s	1990s
road traffic minimal	heavy traffic
felt secure and safe	many places scary and dangerous
never any trouble	lots of gangs
nothing to fear	
lots of bombed buildings	no signs of bombing now
local 'Bobby' respected and 'clipped' naughty children round the ear	children very spoilt
	often badly behaved
less TV	too much TV
smog	cleaner air
no computers or video games	lots of computers and video games

The Four go Travelling
They leave Timmy the dog behind
– The Famous Four go back in time
to the Victorians – Uh Oh!
There's a bomb!
Can the Four solve the mystery?

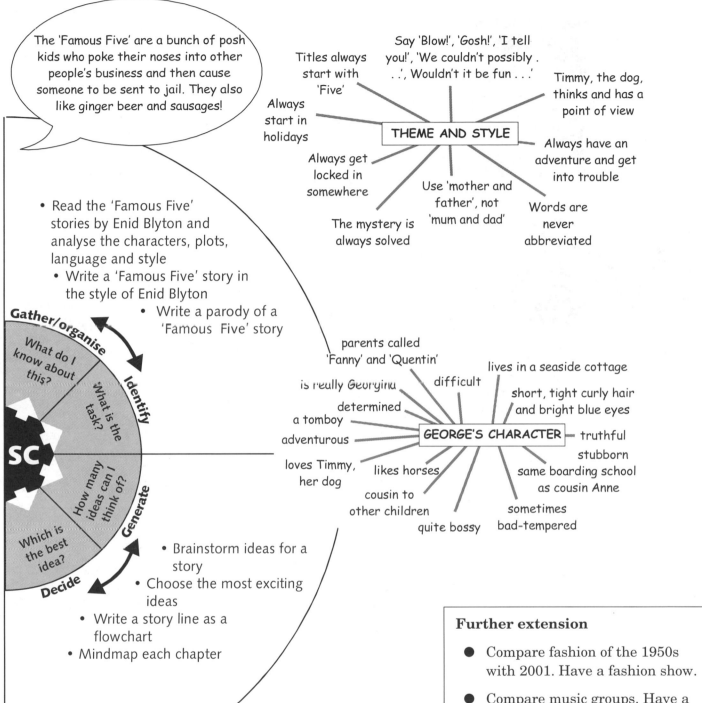

The 'Famous Five' are a bunch of posh kids who poke their noses into other people's business and then cause someone to be sent to jail. They also like ginger beer and sausages!

THEME AND STYLE

- Titles always start with 'Five'
- Always start in holidays
- Say 'Blow!', 'Gosh!', 'I tell you!', 'We couldn't possibly . . .', Wouldn't it be fun . . .'
- Timmy, the dog, thinks and has a point of view
- Always have an adventure and get into trouble
- Always get locked in somewhere
- Use 'mother and father', not 'mum and dad'
- Words are never abbreviated
- The mystery is always solved

- Read the 'Famous Five' stories by Enid Blyton and analyse the characters, plots, language and style
- Write a 'Famous Five' story in the style of Enid Blyton
- Write a parody of a 'Famous Five' story

SC

Gather/organise
- What do I know about this?

Identify
- What is the task?

Generate
- How many ideas can I think of?

Decide
- Which is the best idea?

GEORGE'S CHARACTER

- parents called 'Fanny' and 'Quentin'
- is really Georgina
- determined
- a tomboy
- adventurous
- loves Timmy, her dog
- difficult
- likes horses
- cousin to other children
- quite bossy
- lives in a seaside cottage
- short, tight curly hair and bright blue eyes
- truthful
- stubborn
- same boarding school as cousin Anne
- sometimes bad-tempered

- Brainstorm ideas for a story
- Choose the most exciting ideas
- Write a story line as a flowchart
- Mindmap each chapter

Further extension

- Compare fashion of the 1950s with 2001. Have a fashion show.
- Compare music groups. Have a concert.
- Compare schools. Have a drama production.
- Compare films. Make a powerpoint and video presentation.
- Make a radio programme of 'Then and Now'.

Parody storyline: Five go Rioting

Chapter 1: The Five after SATs Week – *'It's time to do something EVIL!' quivers Julian in a haunting manner.*

Chapter 2: The Five Off on a Riot – *in which the Five riot for many things including 'More sausages and ginger beer in school lunches!'*

Chapter 3: The Five Get Chased – *The Five hide in a Ming vase in an antiques shop. The owners persuade their pursuers not to shoot. 'That was a jolly spiffing close one! exclaims Dick.*

Chapter 4: The Five Get Caught – *An old enemy betrays them to the police. 'Oh no!' said George. 'It seems we won't be home in time for tea!'*

Chapter 5: The Five in the Clink – *By the evening they are all cheesed off with jail life so they plan to send Timmy with a note. However, the dog meets with a nasty end. 'Oh darn!' says George. 'No more sausages or ginger beer for life!'*

This project was devised and implemented by Dick Churchley, Abbey Park Middle School, Pershore, Worcestershire

Artefacts and enquiry: a way to good thinking skills in history

KS2, 2c/d, 3, 4a/b, 5a/b/c

It's difficult to identify different items if you don't recognise them

Valuing artefacts is hard

That artefacts aren't easy to price

Pupils reflect on difficulties of valuing artefacts. Awareness grows of how little some artefacts change over the centuries (e.g. shape of an iron). Awareness of the obsolescence of some artefacts. Why do we stop using some artefacts when they appear so efficient (e.g. bean slicer)? It is fun to learn through artefacts how people lived. Close observation of artefacts reveals history. How would I do this again? Visits to domestic museums/junk shops/antique shops could be a starting point. 'Gatherings from Gran' could be another way in (both artefacts and oral history). Use oral historian in the Identify/Generate stage

Explaining our 'time lines' of bottles and irons made us think carefully and identify changes

Who can we tell?
Sharing their group ideas.
Class discussion with each group demonstrating knowledge of artefact and offering their key questions. Discussion of influences on pricing of their artefact (relevant criteria: demand/age/attractiveness/ 'displayability'/ongoing use)

It was fun choosing items to buy in our 'Bargain Hunt' and then explaining why we bought them

Learn from experience

Communicate

What have I learned?

Let's tell someone!

TA

How well did I do?

Evaluate

Let's do it!

Implement

What have I learned about the artefact?
What would help me next time to learn more? (Contextual pictures/descriptions of use/ reflections of contemporaries who used the artefacts)

Group sharing successful, if some had technical or prior knowledge

Visit to museums often proves beneficial at this stage

We have learnt that some items/artefacts do not change over many, many years

We needed to talk about how we would handle the tasks before we started

Sometimes it is difficult to put artefacts in time order

Complete and consider the grid. Is this complete and what we agree to be our best? Use mentor/teacher to check progress/ideas. Use ICT (Internet/CD-ROM) to access further material. Use reference books, having mind-mapped possible routes for exploration.

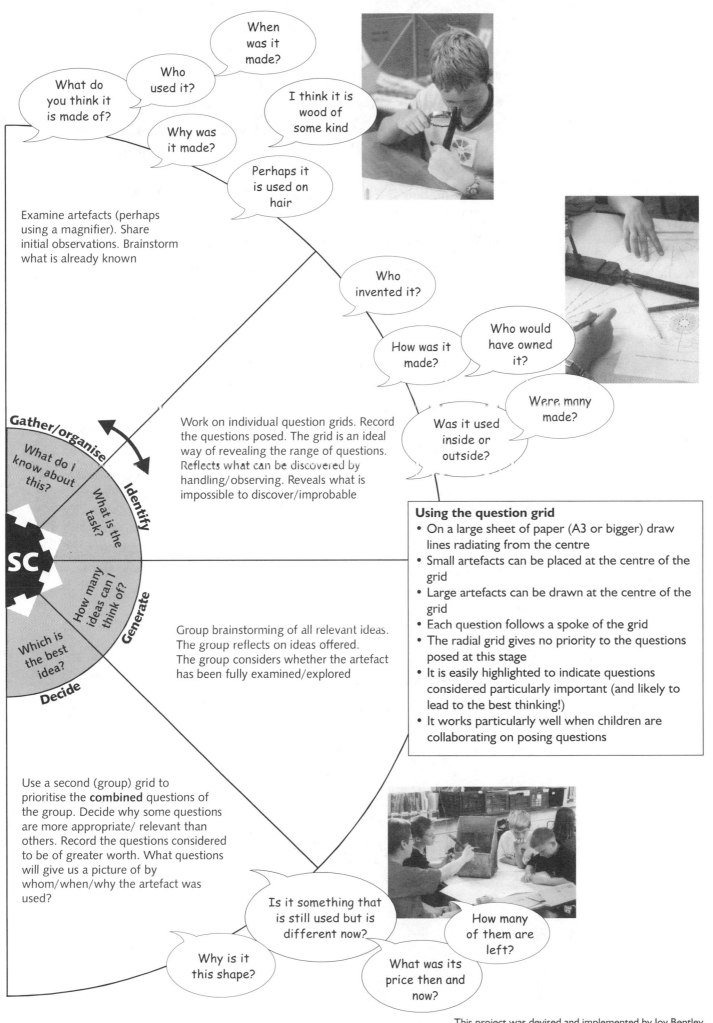

Examine artefacts (perhaps using a magnifier). Share initial observations. Brainstorm what is already known

Work on individual question grids. Record the questions posed. The grid is an ideal way of revealing the range of questions. Reflects what can be discovered by handling/observing. Reveals what is impossible to discover/improbable

Gather/organise
What do I know about this?

Identify
What is the task?

SC

Generate
How many ideas can I think of?

Decide
Which is the best idea?

Using the question grid

- On a large sheet of paper (A3 or bigger) draw lines radiating from the centre
- Small artefacts can be placed at the centre of the grid
- Large artefacts can be drawn at the centre of the grid
- Each question follows a spoke of the grid
- The radial grid gives no priority to the questions posed at this stage
- It is easily highlighted to indicate questions considered particularly important (and likely to lead to the best thinking!)
- It works particularly well when children are collaborating on posing questions

Group brainstorming of all relevant ideas. The group reflects on ideas offered. The group considers whether the artefact has been fully examined/explored

Use a second (group) grid to prioritise the **combined** questions of the group. Decide why some questions are more appropriate/ relevant than others. Record the questions considered to be of greater worth. What questions will give us a picture of by whom/when/why the artefact was used?

This project was devised and implemented by Joy Bentley, Teacher Adviser for Humanities, Worcestershire LEA

Some National Curriculum links

- ● Exploring artefacts promotes the key skills of:

  - – Communication – through responding to a range of sources of information, through discussions, asking and answering questions and presenting findings

  - – Information Technology – using the Internet, CD-ROMs and e-mail for historical enquiry, developing databases

  - – Working with others – on specific historical questions

  - – Improving own learning and performance – through reviewing, setting improvement targets and assessing achievement

  - – Problem-solving – through investigation, decision-making, identifying relevant sources and making conclusions

  - – Thinking skills – processing and evaluating information, describing and explaining events and investigating

- ● The use of artefacts or 'hands-on' activity is *essential for history and the aims for a more inclusive and less prescriptive National Curriculum*

- ● Objects or artefacts (including pictures, objects, documents and people) are specified as a *source for history* which children must have *access* to wherever it is relevant

- ● Remember you only need a *few* artefacts

  - – for promoting the thinking skills and interest of a whole class

  - – for observational drawings

  - – for comparison of then and now

  - – for role play

  - – for historical sequencing

  - – for assessment; this can often be an integral part of the handling experience

  - – for building opportunities for children to pose questions of a variety of artefacts and people

  - – for building links with the recent past and to grasp different interpretations of history

  - – for acquiring historical evidence

Bibliography and Useful Resources

References and further reading

Adams, H. B. (1986) Teaching general problem-solving strategies in the class-room, *Gifted Educational International,* **4**(2), 84–9.

Bentley, R. (1995) Able thinkers learning. *Flying High (now Educating Able Children), Journal of NACE*, Spring, 10–18.

Caviglioli, O. and Harris, I. (2000) *Mapwise.* Stafford: Network Educational Press Ltd.

Cooper, P. and McIntyre, D. (1996) *Effective Teaching & Learning.* Buckingham: Open University Press.

Department for Education and Employment (DfEE) (1999a) *The National Curriculum: Handbook for Primary Teachers in England, Key Stages 1 and 2.* London: DfEE.

Department for Education and Employment (DfEE) (1999b) *The National Curriculum: Handbook for Secondary Teachers in England, Key Stages 3 and 4.* London: DfEE.

Department for Education and Employment (DfEE) (1999c) *The National Strategy Framework for Teaching Mathematics from Reception to Year 6.* London: DfEE.

Department for Education and Employment (DfEE) (2000) *National Literacy and Numeracy Strategies: Guidance on Teaching Able Children.* London: DfEE.

Department for Education and Employment (DfEE) (2001) *Key Stage 3 National Strategy Framework for Teaching Mathematics: Years 7, 8 and 9.* London: DfEE.

Department for Education and Employment (DfEE)/Qualifications and Curriculum Authority (QCA) (1999) *The National Curriculum Handbook for Primary Teachers in England KS1 and 2.* London: DfEE/QCA.

Eyre, D. (1999) *Able Children in Ordinary Schools*. London: David Fulton Publishers.

Gardner, H. (1983) *Frames of Mind*. London: Fontana Press.

Hughes, M. (1994) *Perceptions of Teaching & Learning*. Clevedon: Multilingual Matters Ltd.

Hughes, M. (1999) *Closing the Learning Gap*. Stafford: Network Educational Press Ltd.

Kyriacou, C. (1998a) *Effective Teaching in Schools*. Cheltenham: Stanley Thornes (Publishers) Ltd.

Kyriacou, C. (1998b) *Essential Teaching Skills: Theory & Practice*. Cheltenham: Stanley Thornes (Publishers) Ltd.

McGuiness, C. (1999) *From Thinking Skills to Thinking Classrooms: A Review and Evaluation of Approaches for Developing Pupils' Thinking*. London, DfEE.

National Association for Able Children in Education (NACE)/DfEE Project (1996) *Supporting the Education of Able Children in Maintained Schools*. Oxford: NACE.

National Campaign for the Arts (NACA) (2000) *All Our Futures: A Summary*. London: NACA.

Office for Standards in Education (Ofsted) (1994) *Improving Schools*. London: HMSO.

Office for Standards in Education (Ofsted) (1999a) *Handbook for Inspecting Primary and Nursery Schools* London: HMSO.

Office for Standards in Education (Ofsted) (1999b) *Handbook for Inspecting Secondary Schools* London: HMSO.

Perkins, D. (1992) *Smart Schools: From Training Memories to Educating Minds*. New York: The Free Press.

Raising Standards and Effectiveness Unit (1999) *Autumn Package of Pupil Performance Information*.

Renzulli, J. S. *et al.* (1981) *The Revolving Door Identification Model*. Connecticut: Creative Learning Press.

Scottish Consultative Council on the Curriculum (CCC) (1996) *Teaching for Effective Learning*. Dundee: Scottish CCC.

Scottish Consultative Council on the Curriculum (CCC) (2000) *Direct Interactive Teaching*. Dundee: Scottish CCC.

Siler, T. (1999) *Think Like a Genius Process*. San Fransisco: Berrett-Koehler Communications.

Sternberg, R. J. (1985) *Beyond IQ: A Triarchic Theory of Human Intelligence*. Cambridge: Cambridge University Press.

Sternberg, R. J. and Davidson, J. E. (1986) *Conceptions of Giftedness*. Cambridge: Cambridge University Press.

Stopper, M. (ed.) (2000) *Meeting the Social and Emotional Needs of Gifted and Talented Children*. London: David Fulton Publishers.

Vygotsky, L. S. (1978) *Mind in Society: The Development of Higher Psychological Processes*. Cambridge, MA: Harvard University Press.

Wallace, B. (1988) Curriculum enrichment for all pupils then curriculum extension. *Critical Arts: A Journal for Cultural Studies,* 4(1), 4–5.

Wallace, B. (2000) *Teaching the Very Able Child: Developing a Policy and Adopting Strategies for Provision*. London: David Fulton Publishers.

Wallace, B. (2001) *Teaching Thinking Skills Across the Primary Curriculum: A Practical Approach for all Abilities*. London: David Fulton Publishers.

Wallace, B. and Adams, H. B. (1993) *TASC: Thinking Actively in a Social Context*. Oxford: AB Academic Publishers.

Literacy

Czerniewska, P. (1992) *Learning about Writing – The Early Years*. Oxford: Blackwell.

Dewsbury, A. (1994) *First Steps: Developmental Continuum and Resource Books*. Oxford: Heinemann Educational Books.

Dewsbury, A. (1999a) *Information Text Key Stage 2*, First Steps™ Resource Management, NLS Edition. Oxford: Ginn Heinemann Professional Development (GHPD).

Dewsbury, A. (1999b) *Shared and Guided Reading and Writing at Key Stage 2*, First Steps™ Resource Management, NLS Edition. Oxford: Ginn Heinemann Professional Development (GHPD).

Kent, N. (ed.) (1990) *The Student Writer's Guide: An A to Z of Writing and Language*. Cheltenham: Stanley Thornes.

National Literacy Strategy Activity Resource Banks (1998a) *Module 3 Sentence Level Work*. Oxford: Oxford University Press.

National Literacy Strategy Activity Resource Banks (1998b) *Shared and Guided Reading at KS2*. Oxford: Oxford University Press.

National Literacy Strategy Activity Resource Banks (1998c) *Reading and Writing for Information*. Oxford: Oxford University Press.

Qualifications and Curriculum Authority (QCA) NLS fliers: *The National Literacy Strategy: Grammar for Writing* (ISBN 0 19 312401); *Talking in class* (ISBN 0 19 312296 0); *Engaging all pupils* (ISBN 0 19 312297 9); *Writing in the Literacy Hour* (ISBN 0 19 312299 5); *Writing to inform* (ISBN 0 19 3212300 2).

Rees, F. (ed.) (1996) *The Writing Repertoire: Developing Writing at Key Stage 2*. Slough: National Foundation for Educational Research (NFER).

Wray, D. and Lewis, M. (1995) *Non-Fiction Writing*. Leamington Spa: Scholastic Publications.

Wray, D. and Lewis, M. (1996) *Writing Frames: Scaffolding Children's Writing*. Reading: Reading and Language Information Centre, University of Reading.

Numeracy

Cockcroft, W. H. (1982) *Mathematics Counts: Report of the Committee of Inquiry into the Teaching of Mathematics under the Chairmanship of Dr W. H. Cockroft*. London: HMSO.

Sources of mathematical problems and investigations

Ashworth, F. (1992) *Practical Activities, Investigations and Games (Key Stage 2)*. Devon: Southgate Publishers.

Bolt, B. (1982) *Mathematical Activities: A Resource Book for Teachers*. Cambridge: Cambridge University Press.

Bolt, B. (1984) *The Amazing Mathematical Amusement Arcade*. Cambridge: Cambridge University Press.

Bolt, B. (1985) *More Mathematical Activities*. Cambridge: Cambridge University Press.

Bolt, B. (1987) *Even More Mathematical Activities*. Cambridge: Cambridge University Press.

Bolt, B. (1992) *Mathematical Cavalcade*. Cambridge: Cambridge University Press.

Clarke, B. R. (1994) *Puzzles 4 Pleasure*. Cambridge: Cambridge University Press.

Gardiner, T. (ed.) (2000) *Maths Challenge 1, 2, and 3*. Oxford: Oxford University Press.

Kirkby, D. (1989) *Go Further with Investigations*. London: Unwin Hyman.

Langdon, N. and Snape, C. (1992) *A Way with Maths*. Cambridge: Cambridge University Press.

Murray, J. (1997) *Primary Points of Departure*. Derby: Association of Teachers of Mathematics.

National Numeracy Strategy (2000) *Mathematical Challenges for Able Pupils in Key Stages 1 and 2*. London: DfEE.

Nelson Connect (1999) *Maths Challenges Year 5, Year 6*. Walton on Thames: Thomas Nelson and Sons.

O'Brien, T. (1993) *Problems, Challenges and Investigations*. Colchester: Claire Publications.

Prestage, S. and Perks, P. (2001) *Adapting and Extending Secondary Mathematics Activities*. London: David Fulton Publishers.

Snape, C. and Scott, H. (1992) *How Amazing*. Cambridge: Cambridge University Press.

Snape, Ch. and Scott, H. (1995) *Puzzles, Mazes and Numbers*. Cambridge: Cambridge University Press.

Vout, C. and Gray, G. (1993) *Challenging Puzzles.* Cambridge: Cambridge University Press.

CIRCA, the mathematical magazine, http://members.aol.com/circamaths

A few websites

www.mathsyear2000.org   (this site also has useful links)
www.1000problems.com   (Key Stage 3)
http://nrich.maths.org
http://nrich.maths.org/primary
www.atm.org.uk
www.m-a.org.uk
www.mathsnet.net/puzzles

Science

Beasley, G. and Pengally, B. (1999) *Science Key Stage 1: Scottish levels A–B.* Leamington Spa: Scholastic Publishers.

Department for Education and Employment (DfEE)/Qualifications and Curriculum Authority (QCA) (2000) *Science. Teacher's Guide Update. A Scheme of Work for Key Stages 1 and 2.* London: DfEE/QCA.

Feasey, R. (1999) *Primary Science and Literacy.* Hatfield: Association for Science Education (ASE).

Feasey, R. and Gallear, B. (2000) *Primary Science and Numeracy.* Hatfield: Association for Science Education (ASE).

Feasey, R. and Siraj-Blatchford, J. (1996) *Key Skills: Communication in Science.* Durham: University of Durham.

Goldsworthy, A. (2000) *Raising Attainment in Primary Science* Hatfield: Association for Science Education (ASE).

Goldsworthy, A. *et al.* (2000) *Investigations: Targeted Learning.* Hatfield: Association for Science Education (ASE).

Harlen, W. (1996) *The Teaching of Science in Primary Schools.* London: David Fulton Publishers.

Hollins, M. and Whitby, V. (2001) *Progression in Primary Science.* London: David Fulton Publishers.

Keogh, B. and Naylor, S. (2000) *Starting Points for Science.* Sandbach: Millgate House.

Naylor, S. and Keogh. B. (2000) *Concept Cartoons in Science Education.* Sandbach: Millgate House.

Palmer, P. (ed.) (2000) *Science Challenges: Practical Activities for Able Children.* Hertfordshire: Nuffield Foundation and Hertfordshire County Council.

Qualifications and Curriculum Authority (QCA) (2000) *Standards at Key Stage 2: English, Mathematics and Science.* London: QCA.

ICT

Underwood, J. D. M. and Underwood G. (1990) *Computers and Learning: Helping Children Acquire Thinking Skills.* Oxford: Blackwell.

McFarlane, A. (ed.) (1997) *Information Technology and Authentic Learning.* London: Routledge.

ICT resources

WebQuests related the UK curriculum: www.webquestuk.org.uk
Educational Web adventures: http://www.eduweb.com
Flowol (control software) (free demonstration software downloadable): http://www.data-harvest.co.uk
Inspirations6, TAG Developments Ltd (free demo version downloadable): http://www.taglearning.com
DfES initiative to provide a resource database for more able, gifted and talented pupils: http://www.xcalibre.ac.uk

Index